T0277907

WORLD OF VARIATION

By Mary Otis Stevens
and
Thomas F. McNulty

an i press book   *GEORGE BRAZILLER, INC.* • *NEW YORK*

Copyright © 1970 by Mary Otis Stevens and Thomas F. McNulty.

All rights reserved.

For information, address:

i press incorporated
145 Hanover Street
Boston, Mass 02108
or
George Braziller, Inc.
One Park Avenue
New York, New York 10016

Standard Book Numbers: Cloth—0-8076-0574-3
                       Paper—0-8076-0573-5

Library of Congress Catalog Card Number: 79-129359
First Printing.
Printed in the United States of America.

CONTENTS

Preface   ix

Introduction   xi

PART I   **A FRAMEWORK OF IDEAS**

Chapter 1   **Human Variables**   3

The Problem of Time
The Process of Change
The Visualization of Cultural Forms

Chapter 2   **Human Dimensions**   11

Social Uses of Geometry
Grid Form
Symmetry
Supra-Rational Form

Chapter 3   **Human Adaptations**   17

Land Forms
The Mountain Image
The Web
The Flower Image

Chapter 4   **Human Protections**   24

PART II   **ARCHITECTURE ON A SOCIAL SCALE**

Chapter 5   *Social Concerns*   **29**

The Need for Fantasy
Social Sensitivity
The Idea of Punishment
A Society's Treatment of Nonconformity
A Study of Family Life

Chapter 6   *Communal Innovations*   **45**

The Problem of Connection
Sketch for an American Forum
Group Conflicts
The Belt as a Means of Connection

Chapter 7   *Communal Forms*   **59**

Variation: The Concept of Subsidiary Societies
The Monolith
Growth Rings: An Evolutionary Community

PART III **ARCHITECTURE BEYOND CITIES**

Chapter 8   *Mass Movement and Hesitations*   **67**

The Scale of Mass Movement
Free Action and Collective Movement in Society
The Idea of a "Total Living Space"

Chapter 9   *The Construction of New Societies*   **78**

New Design Scales and Purposes
Societies as Configurations

Chapter 10   **Design of a Linear Society**   **85**

The Concept of Growth Lines
Subdivisions of Growth Lines
Comments on the General Circulation
The Study of Architecture Along the Growth Lines
Government-Cultural Growth Line
Commercial Belt
Heavy Industry
High-Rise Residential Living Units
Dispersed Housing
Divergent Housing Communities
The Segment
Park Belt
Farm Industry Belt
Variation in the Growth Lines
International Growth Lines

Chapter 11   **A Summary of Ideas**   **124**

Notes and References   **127**

Bibliography   **148**

PREFACE

Despite the tyranny and brutality of the present period, one cannot accept its forecast as the future of man. Or else man has no future. All who are involved with and love man, therefore, will try to work for a last chance. The architect-planner can help to visualize the severe problems afflicting most societies today and the new potentialities and purposes that are emerging. Although these hypothetical proposals seldom are realized, they have importance in the alternative directions which they offer a society.

One can begin with a solution and work back to the basic elements of a problem—or one can study images of man and see behind them to needs that have been satisfied in past civilizations and ahead to environments where still unanswered aspects of his nature can be fulfilled. This approach is empirical, based upon the observation that the physical environment, including all its artifacts, accurately records a people. Not only in their record of events but in their arts, the imagination is led to view an emotion or an idea in such a way that a concept becomes apparent. This conceptual world, approached through architecture, is the subject of this book.

To help the reader-viewer perceive the design of the book, Part I articulates the philosophical approaches of the more detailed and specific design projects and ideas in Parts II and III. Design attitudes and purposes are examined for their relevance to both new and already developed world societies. A principal concern of Part I is investigating basic determinants of civilization and speculating upon design frameworks for societies that can absorb growth rates without damaging the sensitive order of environments.

The middle section of the book is involved with present deficiencies in urban environments and how the architect-planner can help compensate with new ideas. Projects are designed within the context and on the scale of existing metropolitan areas, and pertain especially to cities in the United States. The approach was to use their social and cultural conditions for an imagery of environmental change, change not manipulated but regenerative, meaning that the process is internal, evolutionary, inherent in events themselves.

Part III envisages the physical and social definition of whole societies and therefore may be more applicable to nations in their formative stages. Conceptual planning can be more realistically hypothesized for their conditions than for industrial societies like the United States and Western Europe. The design of growth lines for societies in Part III relates to all other parts of the book, often extending the scope of proposals. Like many of the ideas expressed in Parts I and II, the concepts are highly experimental, often originating from intuitions and idealizations.

The design projects and their interrelationships were worked on at intervals over a period of ten years and led us to Ravello, Italy, during the winter and spring months of 1961–1962. Embedded in a wall of a nearby villa was this statement: HUMANUM NIL A ME ALIENUM PUTO, which most neatly describes the authors' viewpoints and their motives for doing the work that follows.

INTRODUCTION

Discussing planning assumptions and attitudes is useful, especially for the new nations of this century which are seeking appropriate forms for their new independence. Many of them were given cultural traditions by the European powers that colonized them. During the next hundred years, however, these colonial frameworks will probably disappear and be replaced by ones more expressive of their nations' inherent cultures. It is important, therefore, that the goals and means for achieving them be determined not only by constitutional doctrines but also by experiments carried out in three-dimensional form by competent architects and planners.

Accordingly, the physical limits and sociocultural scope of the present planning profession are open to question. During the past century technology has altered many basic living patterns so that the newer demands for urban facilities are not likely to be met by traditional procedures. Debate in older cities in the United States about centralized versus decentralized development and the return to or abandonment of their cores illustrates some of the unresolved conflicts.

The city, for example, may not continue to be the most favorable environment in which to locate cultural activities. Significant primarily for commercial and industrial operations, modern cities seldom exploit other human potentialities. Especially when there exist so many alternatives for societies to explore, it may in retrospect turn out to be irrelevant, even self-limiting, to have studied only the points of concentration—the cities—rather than the complete structure of a society.

The change of emphasis in planning may be summarized as being one of scale. Aristotle, for instance, in his treatise *On Civics* noted that, "Ten men are too few for a city, a hundred thousand too many." Certainly the precedent for defining a city in terms of numerical population has ancient roots. Perhaps what really is at issue is the more complicated and sensitive matter of man's collective scales and their influence upon individual and group behavior. A person alone has a unique stature; in a small group of people one has a social relationship and responsive role. In a crowd the individual loses singularity—he becomes a unit, part of a mass. Without understanding these often subtle changes in scale and how population expansion affects social and cultural traditions, many urban environments have been allowed by their inhabitants and administrators to perish or become badly distorted during the past few "explosive" decades. To protect inherent characteristics, cities, like communities of any kind, should be environments where specific activities and usages can be nourished and find identity within a total structure.

An opposite value judgment, which is common to many professional persons involved with urban affairs in the United States, is implied in the assumption that those cities which have the most inhabitants can provide the greatest variety and quality of human experiences. Cities with the largest, most dense, and most heterogeneous populations are for those quantitative reasons considered to be closest to the urban "ideal," and some planning studies forecast future metropolitan areas of twenty-five to fifty million people.

Before such a commitment is undertaken realistically, however, one should consider the range of thought and experience available to the Athenian in the fifth century B.C., to the Roman in the third century A.D., to the Florentine or Venetian during the Renaissance, to the Parisian in the seventeenth century, the Londoner in the eighteenth, and to the Viennese in the nineteenth. Each of these environments was different in physical and social terms, but each stimulated extremely creative artistic, scientific, and intellectual work. What these environments have in common is successful human scale and the attributes of a rich community life. It seems doubtful to try to single out factors such as size and density of a population to describe such indeterminate environmental conditions.

The Technological Approach

Technological innovations also have gradually but pervasively changed planning assumptions and ideals, including those regarding the significance of national wealth. Although cultures have not often flourished without a certain amount of prosperity, and great cultural periods generally have coincided with economic peaks of affluence, one must look closely at the context of these associations before assuming that the wealthier a society becomes, the more significant will be its culture.

The level of prosperity that produced social and cultural advances in past civilizations might be characterized by the society having become self-supporting and able through its superior skills and resources to exert influences upon peripheral peoples.

What seems important today as far as developing sufficient wealth to support an advanced culture is for a society to attain a status in the world market from agricultural products, raw materials, or manufactured goods that can guarantee at least a minimum standard of living to the entire population. This means an economy able to offer full employment, basic health and welfare services, and an above-subsistence income to all inhabitants. Formerly such demands were treated as social fantasies; but they have become practical programs and goals for technologically developed societies.

Technological transformations have changed not only world cultures but also the inspiration for their cultural ideals. Just as painting and sculpture abandoned their past traditions in this century to search for new experiences and means of communication, architecture and planning have sought new roots. In the spirit of the age, they have clustered with the engineering and scientific disciplines and have adopted many of their viewpoints.

The city as a concept is often described as a communication network, as an ideal machine for accommodating a conglomeration of physical and psychological needs, or as some type of organism composed of people, vehicles, buildings, parks, and circulation patterns. Beginning with the affirmative statements of the Futurists and the Bauhaus movement, important conceptual artists have expressed in their works and in manifestos the ambition to make buildings and cities in the image of machines. The architect and planner, then, are thought of as being technicians trained to make environments work efficiently and at a marketable price.

Since these specifications describe a general technological attitude, equally applicable to the manufacture of a car, can opener, or city, apprehension now is expressed generally by those involved with the human environment over the ease with which technological procedures could become an unquestioned method and establish both the theoretical limits and practical controls of every human activity. Probably the foremost fear is that knowledge not capable of calibration or of being programmed for computers would become less and less available to the public. Eventually even a society's thought patterns could be polarized to accord with selected doctrines and techniques. No longer dependent upon nature for inspiration, support, or survival, there is the possibility, too, if such a technocracy were to evolve, that the natural world would be deleted entirely from a culture.

Clearly, changes of this magnitude would alter the human world to the point where few of our present customs and assumptions would still hold. Time may be running out on our options for choosing to continue with or to forego existing, historic frames of reference.

Looking optimistically at the twentieth century's innovations in technology, Buckminster Fuller has made them the basis for his planning and engineering systems. With these and their widest applications he has constructed a "universal" approach to human life. His idealism also has made his vision larger than most of his contemporaries and connects him with the utopian philosophers.

Outline of Planning Assumptions

In the United States, planners and urban designers have been trained to please their clients—in this case developers and city administrators who think in terms of costs and returns on investments as primary factors in decision-making—just as manufacturers of mass consumer goods cater to their buying public. Accordingly the accepted scope of work usually involves making surveys and planning recommendations about critical problems that a community is facing.

The housing shortage, for instance, has involved planners in local, state, and federal agencies, but such experiences have trained the planner to work within limited goals and techniques. Schemes demanding interrelated changes or too much coordination with other agencies, or ones that are involved with far-reaching environmental regeneration have rarely succeeded. To see some improvements accomplished, the planning profession has tended to play a conservative role.

Town planners in Great Britain have found different conditions in the practice of their profession. The national government has been a major client, and the bombings suffered during World War II required whole new cities to be built. Consequently, British planners were given more comprehensive design conditions than their colleagues in the United States. Moreover, England has coped with mass-scale problems for a much longer period than comparably dense regions in North America. Social thinkers such as Ebenezer Howard had turned their attention to urban design in the late nineteenth century. When their ideal schemes, Howard's Garden City concept for instance, were envisioned and sometimes built (two "garden city" prototypes were realized), they expressed attitudes of social benevolence and an eagerness to experiment with planning innovations. Even if most of these utopian projects and their assumptions have proved to be inadequate for twentieth-century conditions, their conceptual approach has persevered in the British planning outlook.

France and Italy also possess a continuity in urban design and planning practices. If at first the Industrial Revolution disrupted their urban plans and patterns, ancient cities such as Paris and Rome appear to have survived the changes of time in a more artful manner than cities of the New World—Chicago, Los Angeles, or New York. In Europe the old cities remain as civic and historic nuclei around which sprawl new satellite towns. Transportation lines have been cut through to prevent the core from suffocating but avenues, squares, parks, and monuments continue to be important symbols of their society's communal life. Le Corbusier's plan for Paris and Pier Luigi Nervi's Autostrada del Sole also illustrate how well their respective cultures can work in scale with contemporary design and planning problems.

Because their programs of economic, social, and cultural development are coordinated, the Scandinavian countries perhaps are closer to being planned societies than any other in this century. They have assumed standardized procedures and equalitarian attitudes. Consequently their organizational structures include total programs of social welfare. Examples of their public housing, town halls, and designs for new and extended areas of existing towns show how a small nation, without unlimited resources or an ideal climate, can utilize its material goods and human talents to their best advantage. Nevertheless, to some observers the comprehensiveness of their planning policies appears restrictive to the individual's freedom of choice, especially if contrasted with the degree of individual decision-making and power exercised by private developers and unrelated planning agencies in the United States.

The people in Finland, Sweden, and Denmark do not however, appear to be deprived of their individuality or of their scope of free action. If their attitude is indicative of future attitudes toward planning, it seems important for new societies to concern themselves now with concepts of order on this scale.

It may be necessary, too, for new nations to distinguish between two different sources of order—one which is imposed upon a society and one which unfolds as a spontaneous expression of its generic character. The problem that appears to be common to most newly founded nations is how to develop and express an intrinsic order while still depending upon and being influenced by larger world powers and their foreign assistance.

Comparisons between the aspirations and characters of various world societies should show how questionable it is for new nations to apply past planning techniques and assumptions to their unique development situations. Because planning decisions can critically affect a society's future, it seems particularly harmful for societies which were not industrialized under nineteenth-century conditions to adopt outdated city forms and planning precepts.

To meet present and future planning challenges requires a skepticism toward older planning procedures and a readiness to try out imaginative hypotheses that relate directly to actual conditions of life in the new societies. This means extending design limits to include generic constructions and processes of environmental change.

PART 1

A FRAMEWORK OF IDEAS

"The most progressive and revolutionary law will remain without application if it is not understood by the people and if the attitudes and habits of the people are contrary to that law."
—Sekou Touré, Guinea, *La Lutte du Parti Democratique de Guinee pour l'Emancipation Africani* (Imprimerie Nationale)

CHAPTER 1

HUMAN VARIABLES

Through the wars and purges of the twentieth century many cultures have been effaced, many peoples have been turned into refugees, many traditions have been overthrown or lost through neglect. It is, in this respect, a time of "deluge." And yet, despite the tyranny and brutality, there are new stirrings in once impassive peoples, new shoots from once dormant cultures. Each ethnic, racial, and national group is now aware of its inherent character and capacities, of its power to assert independence, and of the unique value of its own traditions and history. Reflections upon ideas and destinations for human societies, therefore, are extremely relevant. The erupting energies of peoples and nations, suddenly awakened by the destruction, suffering, and coercions of this century, must be given appropriate social and visual attention before frictions, explosions, and problems of containment provoke a final, desperate destruction.

The Problem of Time

To allow for time—time as a form that the future fulfills —is one of the new tasks of the architect and planner. Concern for the future, however, involves memories of the past and ideals of the present. As a race, men seem to display an inherent desire for permanence, to hold onto the minute that is passing, to preserve the environment that is changing. It seems likely that the process of growth is a sequence of absorption and regeneration, in which society is nourished by—and in turn mothers—new forms of expression.

In designing human environments, different measures of time may be worked with as rhythms identifying the scale of experiences happening within an individual's life span and those dimensioning a cultural phase.

Religious communities (both ancient mystical cults like the Essenes and contemporary Christian and Buddhist monasteries) have expressed ideal images of time in the architecture of environments created for private and communal worship. Political ideologies also rely upon scales of time to achieve their long-term objectives. The doctrine of historical determinism has been applied in Marxist societies to "five-year plans" and in this reference, it is interesting to imagine how societies emerging from long periods of foreign domination will use time as a framework for their ideals.

The Process of Change

The paradox seems to be in allowing for change, and yet designing for the abstraction that does not change.

Brasilia and Chandigargh are examples of twentieth-century cities that have been designed to be in scale with the accelerating process of cultural change. The risk in making such social experiments is that if the solutions are arbitrary, they are not likely to work; that is, inhabitants of the new environments lose the security of the past without gaining the stimulation expected from a future-oriented design idea.

It seems probable that choosing what is to be changed and what is to become permanent in a society

is the slow work of cultural traditions. Those innovations which are in line with the cultural phase are strengthened, while those moving in antithetical directions are forced away by the motion of the mainstream. Nevertheless, these waiting forces often become valuable as historical alternatives, as repositories of their society's unused potentialities.

Therefore, an appropriate way of denoting the skeleton of the American society (originally intended to be a system of checks and balances) may be by an abstract imagery of vector forces. Abstractly one

6

visualizes various factions countering and aligning with each other until a resultant direction is determined. Each vector, having both magnitude and direction, may be assumed to be an active thrust that achieves its purpose until some of its components deflect to competing forces. The society's development, consequently, does not suggest a continuous straight line; instead it may be more truthfully denoted by a series of relatively short, energetic segments that forge a historical direction.

Psychologically, it may be healthy that most individuals are not often conscious of the cultural direction which moves them in its path. Being both independent from and yet parasitically bound to it, the individual's role may resemble a barnacle's in attaching to the culture. Only during critical periods are individual and collective concerns in a society likely to be identical.

Furthermore, within short time intervals the continuity and pervasiveness of sociocultural forces may not appear to be as strong as they actually are. In the American society decisions often represent expedient power plays among temporary although forceful factions, but these very likely include also "grass root" strength of popular attitudes and traditions. In this association they are elements of the cultural framework.

Change, therefore, does not justify wasteful eradication of the past. Is it not from desperation that a person or a society destroys all vestiges of variation?

The Visualization of Cultural Forms

To protect their identity and independence as a society, earlier communities enclosed meaningful social, religious, and cultural practices within a protected boundary. The temenos, acropolis, and city wall were built for defense; but like the towers of San Gimagnano, they also were strong visual forms that gave identity to the people of the society. Towers, ziggurats, obelisks, triumphal arches, and so on, can be interpreted as monumental sculptures symbolizing their societies. In some examples, such as the evolution of the Doric, Ionic, and Corinthian Orders in temple architecture, a refinement of proportion is achieved which endures as an aesthetic standard for succeeding centuries and civilizations.

The strength of the cultural forms seems to rely upon public attitudes and belief. Not surprisingly then, many lose their power to communicate. A good example is the "Tree of Liberty," an extremely provocative symbol during the American Revolutionary period but now

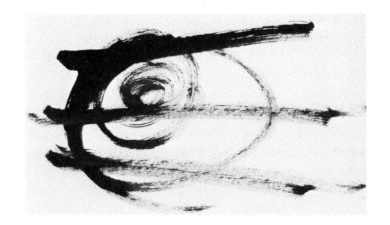

merely a historical reference. An interesting contrast is the British crown. That symbol still works because, like the monarchy it represents, contemporary meanings overlay its ancient imagery.

CHAPTER 2

HUMAN DIMENSIONS

The limits of what is "possible" and what is "impossible" seem to have been set by man himself acting through his social and cultural traditions. Ceremonial rites and taboos have been identified by Jung, among others, as being symbolic forms which, besides depicting routines of life in the tribe, attempt to define and set limits for the human world. Anthropological studies reveal also how basic human uncertainties have evolved through various cultures to show refinements and improvisations completely unforeseen in their primitive states.

Perhaps the original incentive for fabricating and dimensioning human environments was man's physical and psychological insecurity. Men have built civilizations on cliffs, in water, on flat plains, in the desert, in tropical temperatures, and in the Arctic regions of this planet. Civilizations have thrived or failed where living conditions were difficult and also where they have been relatively easy.

It appears obvious, too, from looking at a number of civilizations that some human traits are more valuable than others in producing an enduring society. For example, the ability to organize; one can see it as the cornerstone of Roman civilization. Roman clarity and order are evident in the forums of its cities and colonial settlements; in its legal, monetary, postal, and irrigation systems; in examples of its transportation and engineering work; and in the great social and visual scales on which projects were undertaken over centuries. Roman civilization may have been a rare achievement in man's total history, but it testifies to the potential power and stability of a society with a great capacity and liking for order.

Forming visual languages, even at the most primitive stages of digging forms in a landscape, seems to be a spontaneous human activity. Pythagoras began the tradition of associating geometrical proportion with musical harmony. Concepts of beauty, then, could be translated into quantitative terms and, like the gardens designed by Le Nôtre for Louis XIV's court, identified with a social order. Emerging from these roots, architecture as an art and engineering science still holds in its traditions many of these early associations. A spirit of wonder pervades its treatises and rules of proportion from Vitruvius' *Ten Books on Architecture* to Le Corbusier's *Le Modulor*.

Social Uses of Geometry

Architects also have used geometry to articulate their moral thoughts about society. Originating with the "City of God" concept, Utopias have been visualized in a tradition of abstract geometric imagery to distinguish them from the actual environmental conditions of their time.

Despite the obvious differences between static societies of the past and the mobility and fast-changing patterns so characteristic of the present, geometry still can be useful in visualizing conceptual sociocultural situations. Contemporary applications of geometry need not exhibit the rigidity of earlier environmental concepts, but as abstractions could stimulate new design ideas and approaches.

Grid Form

The grid form has been one of the oldest and most general methods of superimposing a human order upon nature. Greek and Roman colonies employed the grid to establish their rule and culture upon new territories quickly and efficiently. The Cartesian system of co-ordinates, the compass points, the directional terms "up," "down," "right," "left," are everyday idioms. The grid is the pattern of the sidewalk, the roadway, highway, rail lines—the majority of lines that man has etched upon the earth's crust.

Cities are laid out in grid lines; the grid form defines the circulation of people and vehicles; it determines the size and scale of buildings and the systems of services feeding them.

The "grid of the earth" can be viewed from the air. Over the western plains for perhaps a thousand miles the huge tracery of ten-, twenty-, or hundred-mile grid patterns lie below—straight, accurate, unbroken. Rivers and arid land cut in angles across the grid planes, but they are never strong enough to destroy them. Cities or villages always appear at intersections of grid lines.

Grid of the earth

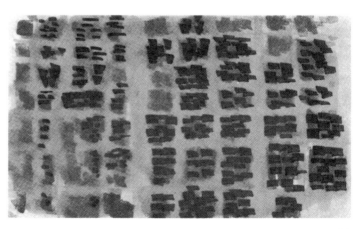

13

This occurrence tacitly states that man seeks an order, his own order, and will impose it on any scale wherever he explores or settles. Where men have not been, one does not find the grid. Undelineated patterns are symbols of man's absence, not presence.

As a future possibility, the grid pattern points the way for inclusive geometries to evolve from and give form to entire societies.

Symmetry

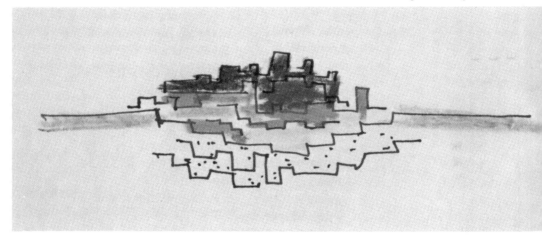

Symmetry has helped men to encompass the complex functions of cities and provide significant locations for the most meaningful shrines and monuments in their cultures. The temple, mosque, church, the palaces of kings—all these building types illustrate how symmetry was used to show perfection and omnipotence in the human environment.

Symmetry has been used to denote the desired order in "utopian" societies. Through symmetry, geometric

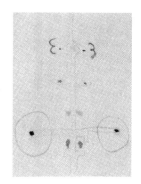

forms can be simplified to state clearly a designated purpose. In contrast to actual living conditions, symmetrical relationships suggest the wholeness and serenity, the nearness to perfection of idealistically constructed environments.

Used in new architectural associations, symmetry might become a means of relating outer forms to their inner psychological associations. Just as the internal structure of things, their essences, were the subject of Mondrian's and Klee's paintings, so can they be an architect's preoccupation—images mirroring images, ideas of rhythms and repetitions. These suggest interior qualities latent in spaces and forms. They imply a correspondence between what is seen and what is reflected or hidden from view. Positive and negative affirm their opposite—as seen in Arp's or Henry Moore's sculptures, and as observed by Jung in the conscious and unconscious expressions of the psyche.

When allowed to meander, the line creates both area and volume which we recognize but cannot identify with classical notions of geometric forms. These "free" innovations of contemporary architecture are determined by new laws and techniques, or may be intuitions of the artist.

Free form is a new, supra-rational geometry belonging more to the future than to the past. Its uses and laws of proportion are not yet all discovered. Nonetheless, this thought is offered: To see within space, to be inside form and color is the new destination of architecture.

**Supra-Rational
Form**

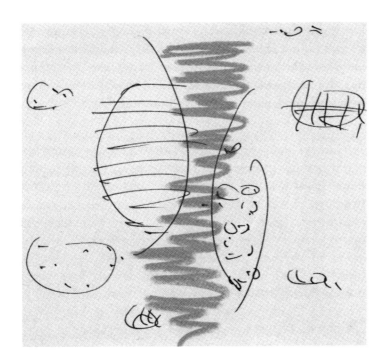

The internal structure
of things

CHAPTER 3

HUMAN ADAPTATIONS

The world of nature seems to be inherently related to men's psychic needs. It has inspired an imagery— African totem forms, gargoyles on the parapets of Gothic cathedrals, the dancing spirits that guard Indian temples, and the famous Egyptian Sphinx—that merges characteristics of the human and natural worlds. And just as geometry has been a means of giving physical measure and order to their environments, nature and concepts from nature have provided men with sources of fantasy. Venice and Amsterdam are two such masterfully designed cities. The interstices of their canals provide a basic visual organization of spaces and circulation that is harmonious with the functions served by the society. The human world, then, becomes a superposition over the natural one; in Venice particularly, the water becomes a magnificent surface of reflection for all the forms and activities of the city, which become fantasies of color, sculpture, and architecture that float like spontaneous images over the water.

Although their economic dominance has ended, both Venice and Amsterdam have continued to be important cultural centers. Their complete integration with the experience of nature gives them an enduring, timeless attraction. In contrast, most American cities, hardly over a hundred years old, have already lost whatever natural features or views may have originally supplied a character and orientation to their environments. Without an inherent identity or focus for their development, they offer few aesthetic or physical pleasures to present or future inhabitants. Social planners might have foreseen this possibility had they been fully aware of the need for nature, with its enduring forms and processes, in man-made environments, and of the need in men to connect their relatively brief, inconsistent, and self-centered patterns to the time scale and order of the natural world.

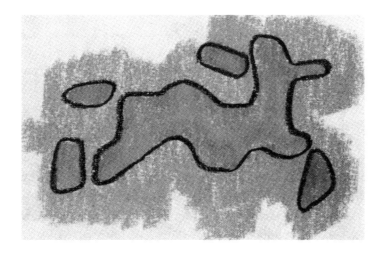

Landscape designs show in what elemental ways men can make forms, and in so doing create human environments. A sensitivity in handling land forms can give a correct scale and character as well as a pleasantness to living in any environment, regardless of its size and other human qualifications. Perhaps because of the standardization in the products of industrialized societies, there appears to be a uniformity in the size and character of most urban environments. The only

Land Forms

way to avoid this depressing monotony is by making provisions for environments to relate to natural land forms.

A contemporary view of land is from the air. Large-scale forms of lakes, mountains, and highway patterns become visual elements comparable to building facades and the urban landscape seen from ground views. Light patterns at night looking down on cities such as Chicago make a mystery out of crude, cluttered day realities. Much of the ugliness visible from the ground becomes obliterated by distance. As buildings and levels of living become more vertical, this aspect of site designing increases in significance.

Many societies, too, are contending with unusual land forms in their plans for expansion. Siberia, the Sahara Desert, Alaska, and nothern Canada are several regions in which actual settlements are being proposed and experimented with under environmental conditions once considered too marginal for ordinary human life.

However, it may be desirable for certain kinds of forms to be left in their natural state because of the human hardship in developing them, or because they are useful buffers between conflicting societies. Switzerland, for example, has been able to protect its independent development in the midst of stronger and aggressive European neighbors by means of its ring of mountain ranges. For centuries England was able to hold itself remote from continental Europe by its Channel; and the colonial independence of the United States was aided by its two oceans.

Particular land forms that men have never influenced or subdued have become perhaps for that reason, symbols of awe and curiosity.

Before technological skills become so advanced that natural barriers and conditions will no longer be significant, it may well be desirable to select some land areas in the world to be free of human settlement. Mountains such as the Matterhorn and Mount Everest, deserts such as the Gobi and the Sahara, and glacial regions of the Arctic and Antarctic are environmental barriers that men have challenged. These might be considered the territories, the images that, belonging to all men, should remain unpossessed.

The mountain form is associated with man's aspirations and with his idealism. The God of the Hebrews spoke from Mount Sinai and the Greeks placed their gods on Mount Olympus and their Muses on Mount Parnassus.

The Mountain Image

As well as being the locus of great insights, the mountain image is also a source for images of the unattainable and mysterious. The ziggurat, dome, steeple—all these sacred forms of man's civilizations are reminiscent of the mountain's peak. So is the sky-scraper, but its image is misused by men dedicated to increasing the prestige of banks, soap companies, and the like. It becomes an arrogant intrusion into older environments, making earlier landmarks appear insignificant and destroying generic relationships.

Even cities of towers like New York have distorted the mountain's imagery. When men build, therefore, they should understand these unconscious associations and not permit their towers, rising like mountain slopes above ordinary and utilitarian functions, to be converted to trivial purposes.

The Web

The web as an image of nature offers disguise. It is a form of protection and penetration that can apply to problems of connection and isolation in human environments. A city, for example, while still providing all requirements for privacy, might be designed as a web that would penetrate and weave together the lives of all its inhabitants. This image of a web, however, should not be compared with the jumble of present urban areas. Like the spider, architects and planners must draw the threads and visualize the webs in man-made environments.

The web as a human construction could be visible and invisible—a framework that would be assumed to become denser as it developed—encompassing systems and people without restricting their free movements.

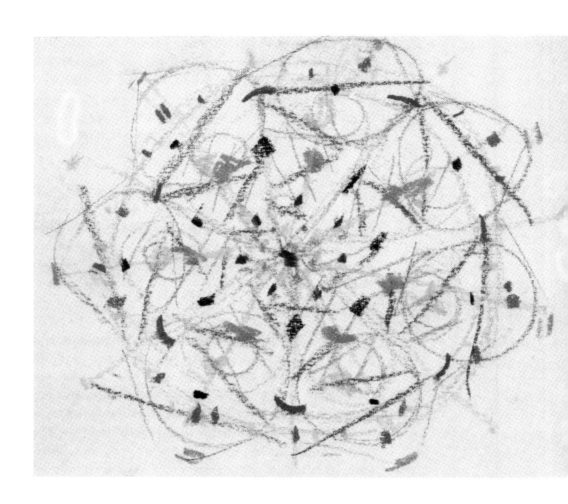

The flower is an image of beauty. Its form is symmetrical and delicate and reminiscent of the mysterious process of life unfolding from a seed. These often are qualities in works of art. They might be useful, too, in environments planned to expand and change with time. The designer should remember the methods of nature in working with development projects so that at all stages of their materialization they will be balanced and guided by an innate plan of growth.

Unlike the fate of flowers, man's civilizations do not seem to be predestined to a sequence from origin to decay; but they appear to be even more precarious than flowers in their history of survival. Yet later societies bloom from their roots, so that the ruins of civilization remind one of the seeds of flowers. In the Western world, the Greek and Roman cultures have re-seeded themselves and enriched all societies after them by pervading the present with their past mystery.

The Flower Image

CHAPTER 4

HUMAN PROTECTIONS

Architects and planners involved with new concepts of freedom and order can help give a balance and serenity to human environments to contend with people's fears and anxiety. A typical need for psychologically designed and protected environments is in congested urban and industrial regions such as the Northeastern Seaboard of the United States. Social and visual forms distinguishing between different time rates and pressures would prevent the machine pace from imposing an unnecessary hurry upon neighboring residential environments and the occupations of leisure time.

On a larger scale, the concept of transitional zones might include ways of distinguishing between what is of permanent and temporary value in a culture. The task is to create environments that are open in the sense of being capable of absorbing new information and hypotheses, and of relating innovations to fruitful traditions of a society. Superimposing activities, even whole communities, upon one another without creating social frictions or a visual clutter are the design implications from the idea of human protections.

The way that animal species coexist in all geographic and climactic regions by conforming to different strata and methods of survival is suggestive of

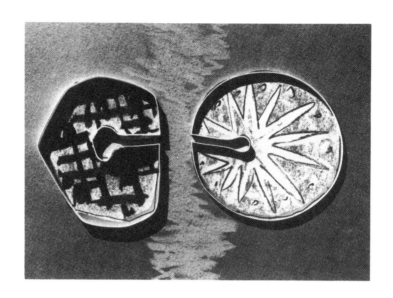

the superimposed human worlds that men could build. Contrast and variety could be fostered in their development by using psychological as well as physical controls in planning.

Furthermore, physical designs can begin to express the new dimensions of space—space defined in terms of galaxies, light years, and velocities which were only suppositions in the recent past—but a person must be at ease before this scale of social and visual relationship is enjoyable. Environments in the future may demand this kind of human protection.

PART II

ARCHITECTURE ON A SOCIAL SCALE

"The city teaches the man."

Simonides, 556–467 B.C.

CHAPTER 5

SOCIAL CONCERNS

Just as Oscar Wilde advised himself as poet to seek only the most tragic moments in life, the architect and social designer also should seek out and study areas of misery within a culture.

Study the human being in three dimensions. What are the basic stimulants that make him live? What thwarts his growth and malforms him psychologically? How do visual impulses affect psychological impulses? What are proper safeguards in a culture?

Consider, for instance, the pressures that drive people into loneliness, into the walled caves of their secret structures, where illusions feed on fears and substitute for former real companionships. Beginning with the first act of shutting out the world and retreating into the solitude of a single room, a person can gradually become lost from his fellows. Not until these hidden cavities of loneliness have been opened up are many people made aware of how inhuman some of their environments have become.

By relieving conditions that cause breakdowns and crime, and by more sensitively integrating reform and rehabilitation institutions with a society's customary living patterns, many currently critical social problems might be avoided. Deteriorated sections of a city, for example, reflect an attitude of not caring, not only on the part of the inhabitants but also on the part

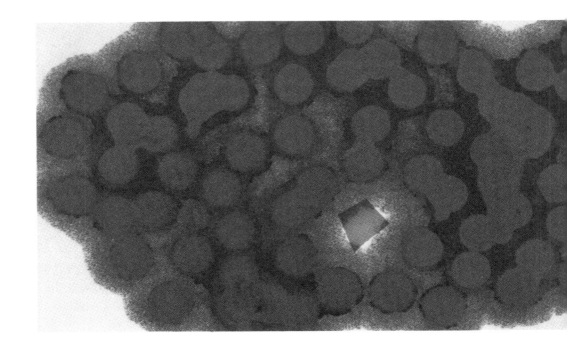

of the total community. People living in blighted neighborhoods sense the lack of concern, which can only aggravate their antisocial behavior. Eradicating an area, however, does not remove the presence of the fears and desperation which many of the tenants hold within themselves. In fact, outer conditions of decay may be sought out by and be a solace to people psychologically frustrated or withdrawn.

Not everyone is capable of living in an environment of truth.

The Need for Fantasy

Architecture as an art form could initiate auxiliary constructions that replenish environments with balance and serenity—not to divert the individual from his private sufferings as much as to help him cope with the demands of his society. Also, to remain sensitive the human being requires aesthetic enjoyments, whether found by the senses or the intellect, whether it is beauty appreciated in man-made or natural objects, or in artistic or scientific concepts.

The need for beauty as a social oasis

Artists may see how to use fantasy to answer a society's need for disguise. Industrial societies in particular could use expressions of fantasy to alleviate unbearable strains in environments where intense energies and nerve strain are generated.

Controlled circulation can be designed as a transitional experience to diminish antagonisms between

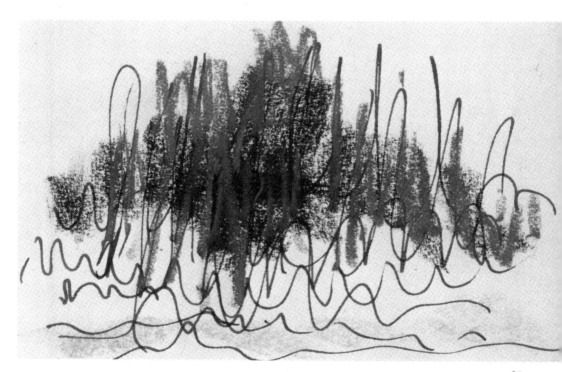

31

environments markedly different in character and tempo. Through pauses and interim diversions, a filtering movement also protects sensitive points within environments from undergoing internal conflicts.

Likewise, there could be spaces designed for explosions in a society, for pulsations to release their repressed energies without destroying people or life functions. Fireworks, one of the most imaginative expressions of vicarious emotions, can be used also, as in Paris on Bastille Day, to achieve a social purpose. Comparable to fireworks as a concept of fantasy were the late nineteenth-century balloon voyages and their sequels in the twentieth century, the man-made satellites, are attracting a similar attention.

In the future, societies may use psychologically designed forms and activities to provide relief from higher cultural standards and their accompanying restraints upon behavior. Except for advertising purposes the visual-psychological impact of symbols used everyday in our society has hardly been explored.

The filtration concept applies to environments in which there is a need to separate conflicting social and visual patterns or to prevent aggressive intrusions

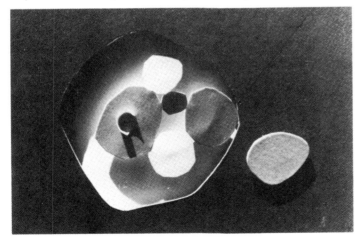

There can be forms and spaces that are understood only through the unconscious

Furthermore, it can be asked: Should we always design for the normal person? Why does an environment fail for the abnormal? Is abnormality fostered by too much or by too little environmental stimulation?

Social Sensitivity

Consciously or through custom, societies choose their social and cultural commitments. Some, such as the United States, believe that government should intrude as little as possible into social and cultural affairs in order to safeguard the individual's liberty; while others, notably the more recently established nation-states in Africa and Asia, espouse broad programs of social and cultural welfare.

The scope of an individual's responsibility to society and the extent to which society is obligated to fulfill a person's nonmaterial, in addition to obvious physical, needs are issues underlying many contemporary confrontations and national ideologies. They are particularly visible in instances of extreme need, such as in the kind of commitments that are made to disturbed, defective, and criminal members of a society.

Although punitive and therapeutic functions are common to all societies, it is surprising that not more is known about how oppressive or permanently damaging the visual character of confined environments may be to those interned. Even worse, the bleak buildings of prisons and mental hospitals in the United States express hostility and rejection, feelings which the society shows in other ways as well toward its deviating members.

The Idea of Punishment

Whether there should be prisons or mental hospitals at all can be investigated most easily by societies that have not already built hundreds or thousands of each.

33

The glass wall

Because of public unconcern, however, alternate types of protection and rehabilitation that might replace these institutions are seldom explored.

Moreover, in an extremely balanced society there might not be any institutions as such, but simply areas where persons unable or unwilling to conform to the society's "norms" would be supervised in their movements and relationships, yet could still remain within the general society. The sketch shows a prison environment that is related to society but separated from it by a thin membrane of protection. The inmate would be able to work and live with his family under the guidance of trained personnel.

The absence of a punitive character is the strongest suggestion in this idea. For persons who cannot live freely in society without injuring themselves or others, a restricted environment may be necessary, but the character of this confinement should neither convey a lack of respect for the patient or prisoner nor isolate him from friends and family.

Most prisons for men and women in the United States are influenced in their design by the underlying belief that criminals must repay in suffering the amount of injury which they once inflicted upon someone else. The taking of one life demands the destruction of another. Although capital punishment gradually is being abolished, the sentence of "life imprisonment" is not much more humane. The negative step of not physically killing the criminal should not be mistaken for a charitable and enlightened public attitude.

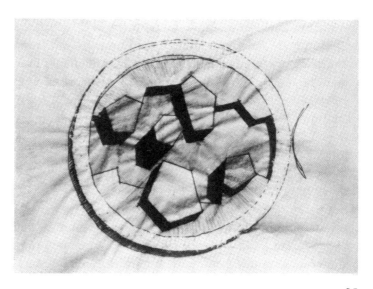

The security wall

The environments in which most persons must spend a life sentence are so psychologically unhealthy that there is little hope of reforming their antisocial attitudes. Usually an inmate's hostility only increases from experiences that happen within the prison environment. Consequently, the return of freedom becomes merely a return to former associates and destructive acts until the person is again caught, retried, and resentenced.

In the United States, the expense, waste of life, and unnecessary suffering endured by both the society and the criminal are enormous, but the public, except when prison riots attract a sporadic attention, has not been sufficiently aroused to demand important changes.

Generally belonging to the most insecure economic and cultural groups, most criminals are prepared for their life in crime by the neighborhoods in which they were born. Lacking social stability, cultural orientation, and usually an adequate education, and suffering from feelings of personal inadequacy and hostility one can be easily tempted by destructive outlets. A person in committing acts against the law becomes an outsider to the general society, but gains identification with an isolated and closely knit community replacing it. Other relationships ensue after the criminal is arrested. Although still considered by one's associates to be part of the gang, by the society one is viewed as a possible member again—conditionally, upon paying penance, serving "time." And to arbitrators and enforcers of the society's justice, the criminal exemplifies weakness and evil. Those who are most involved with the efforts that a society expends for its protection, like policemen who symbolize social restraints and for that reason often become special targets of criminal acts, understandably demand the severest penalties and the harshest treatment of prisoners.

The trial, which can be interpreted as a counterposing of these relationships, is the most publicized aspect of crime and punishment in a modern society. As the pivotal figure, the person standing trial becomes both observer and partaker in the process of justice. Perhaps because of the trial experience, many criminals spend their time in prison studying criminal law, especially aspects pertaining to their particular case which might warrant a new trial or become grounds for an appeal. In some cases these efforts are rightly motivated, but for many criminals their refusal to accept guilt probably derives from psychological factors within their own personalities.

Fundamentally, then, a prison experience should be designed to bring about the reformation of basic social attitudes, most optimistically by the inmates finding new meaning and orientation for their lives. Under such circumstances a prison sentence is not utterly futile "marking time." Also, if genuinely rehabilitated, an ex-con is unlikely to revert to former antisocial activities and associates upon his reentry into society, and accordingly no longer poses a social threat. Conversely, the high rate of return to prisons in the United States after release or parole points up the lack of rehabilitation in prisons under the present system.

Expressing an evolutionary prison concept, the sketch stresses the change of character between the guarded cells and the more casual environments in which inmates meet with their families and friends in relative privacy, learn new skills in workshops, spend their earnings in stores, participate in physical recreation, and develop intellectual interests through libraries, art exhibitions, and auditorium programs.

The wall is thought of as a protective barrier shielding the prisoners from a hostile society as much as giving the society a sense of security. The wall should not convey hostility, however. It could become exciting through penetrations and projections making a sculpture out of the circumferential elevation.

The design clearly separates the punitive experiences of confinement and isolation which are identified with the wall, and the rehabilitation process represented in activities occurring in the free center. The prisoner would begin his sentence within the security wall. As he progressed in his social reformation he could be allowed more contacts with his fellow inmates, family, and friends—events primarily associated with the central spaces. Eventually a prisoner would leave the security area entirely and spend the remaining portion of his sentence in transitional environments. The inside area of the prison becomes, therefore, a bright spot, an incentive for the prisoner to begin the process of rehabilitation.

A larger prison complex might have other communal functions, including living and working provisions for the families of prisoners. In this sketch model the prison is intended to be a focal point in a community accessible from all points around the circumferential wall and penetrated by two main avenues.

Within the prison itself the main circulation route is a mall meandering through the core of buildings to attract the outside public and encourage its participation in social activities. The prison's interior environment contrasts with its security section by placing the visual and social emphasis on community experiences.

An effort, too, is made to obtain privacy in areas for therapy, education, and leisure. To emphasize the individuality and privacy of these spaces, light within the retreat areas could be controlled through roof openings rather than by the usual wall fenestration.

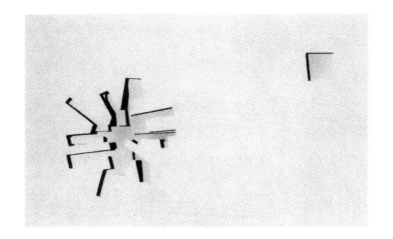

The model is an expression of an internal explosion with a restricted environment

Following this approach further, why not try to structure activities and experience in prisons from the inmates' point of view, beginning with their rejection of standard social attitudes and responses? With this understanding, the architect might work with spaces, forms, textures, and color in prison environments in order to provoke and release the repressed anger and hatred disturbing many prisoners.

Abstractly, the crack becomes a limited form of escape, a forceful release from the confined routines of prison life, and, at least subconsciously, it could be recognized as such by the prisoners. Penetration into a prison's dense interior spaces could be dramatized further by strong uses of color and by the shadows cast by the jagged edges and contrasting planes.

The explosion represents the destructive tendencies in each prisoner, transformed into a design that uses those energies to build a new order.

Perhaps from an evolutionary viewpoint persons in a society who fall outside established norms can be classified as rejects—the leftovers from the struggle for survival. Because the outward signs of inner disturbances or nonconformity can be repugnant to many members of a society, those who deviate are cast out as social misfits. As human beings, however, they and their needs merit serving with as much respect as any other segment of a society. Besides, extreme eccentricity is not just symptomatic of an individual's lack of social adjustment, but shows even more painfully the neglect of a society in providing this person with sufficient human fulfillment.

Unlike previous forms of social organization, an advanced technological culture does not confer a traditional status upon men and women, nor define orthodox procedures for educating the young. Consequently roles and standards of behavior cannot be uniform.

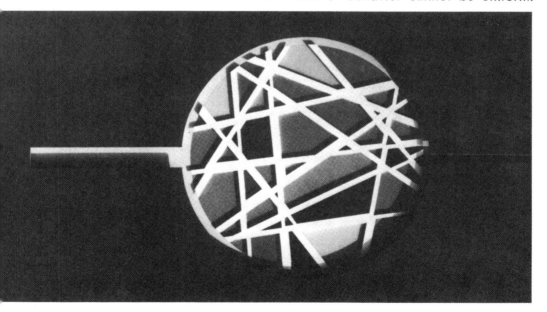

Also social deviation seems to follow a historical precedent of intensifying when a culture begins to encourage variation from its earlier precepts. A nonconforming group often reveals, even by caricature, basic weaknesses in a society's fundamental relationships, and can perform, therefore, a creative function through its rejection of established norms.

With this awareness, the experimental architect, educator, and social planner might examine the social needs and relationships of people whose behavioral patterns do not fall within a society's acceptable limits. Environmental proposals which are mentioned here suggest a way of relating these nonconforming activities to the mainstream of life in an urban society.

Since the customs of a nonconforming minority are

Superposition of living patterns

usually unrelated, if not hostile to the surrounding society, their environment is shown in this sketch model to be a self-contained form which abruptly breaks away from existing urban patterns.

This design suggests an encompassing balance, ostensibly on a city's scale, between nonconforming, even abnormal deviations (identified here with the random circulation on the raised circulation levels) and the inconspicuous, yet more massive cultural influence of conventional environments. The superposition not only separates and safeguards differences between discordant groups, but as an image it proposes new options and design experiences for a society.

A Study of Family Life

Despite strains and conflicts, the family appears to be the most enduring and basic social unit. Perhaps versatility is its most favorable feature. In different historical and cultural contexts, the structure of family life has varied in manner of kinship, in methods for training the young, and in traditional roles assigned to members. For example, a farm family through extensive interrelationship can grow to be a considerable social, economic, and political nucleus, and therefore exert real power in community affairs. Moreover, the structure of rural and town governments, like the New England town meeting, often reflects the system of authority exercised within the family unit itself.

Unlike its rural predecessor, however, the family unit in industrial environments is not likely to be deeply rooted in past traditions nor as well related to a community's contemporary development. Children rarely follow their parents into occupations, and as a result do not depend upon older family members for their schooling, or even for social and cultural leadership.

Mobility is another transforming influence on family life. In an industrial society changed economic conditions and easy means of transportation attract families from their native regions to distant localities. Disrupted by moving, a family is then likely to need guidance in coping with problems of adjustment.

Another strain on the family unit is reworking its role from the vantage point of pervasive twentieth-century revolutions. Despite the recommendations of Freud and others that society is most enriched by efforts of people who are motivated by a detached human compassion, the family, with its essentially introverted structure, predictably will remain centered around its primary members.

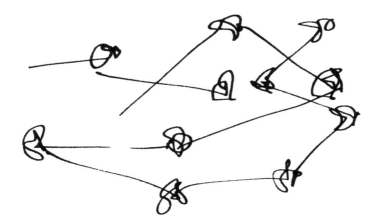

Family movement

Variations of this conflict between personal objectives and community responsibility are likely to preoccupy the future. Balances between communal and private demands in a family's development inevitably become concerns for the planner and architect. What type of spaces, for instance, should be designed to satisfy the strong desires for privacy and individuality within a family nucleus; and what kind of community movement and interaction can be accepted by a group of families?

Sketch of a visual community

Imagining that a social community is also a visual community, and expressing the rhythms of private and communal spaces, can bring about revisions in residential environments and in the family structure itself.

CHAPTER 6

COMMUNAL INNOVATIONS

Unlike the workings of nature, cities of men do not, by changing and expanding, maintain a proportional growth. At best, human plans and decisions, no matter how patiently worked upon or creatively inspired, appear crude and fallible in comparison with the innate processes of nature. There are no chromosomes, no cells, no organic methods of structure to incorporate new elements.

Fortunately, one compensation can be given by rich overlays of time—in the imagery and points of connection between past and present living patterns—and how they are reflected in a city's forms and spaces. An environment that has absorbed a variety of historical periods and social directions becomes an exciting experience. Moreover, the scale and character of past happenings often inspire future innovations, so that a continual reseeding connects past to future and future to past. As in Rome, memorabilia from the past and utterances of the present are seen within one context making an "eternal city."

If, however, past episodes are not well integrated with a city's current uses, their presence in new environments tends to promote clutter and discord. Without realizing how new social functions will join to an existing social and cultural order, new purposes and buildings may not be improvements; in fact they can influence environments adversely by clashing with native traditions and original design impulses.

Although not always recognized, the scope of an idea implicitly is given in the design, which suggests the further speculation that it may be particularly this salient vision that enables skillful architects and planners, acting like the chromosomes of the body, to give even such complex environments as cities a continuing order and human scale.

In this regard, what appears to be lacking in industrial cities like many in the United States is a generic process for growth and change. Clearly the crisis in these cities cannot be explained by external events as plausibly as by their failure to resolve inner conflicts, by their neglect of culture, and by sporadic expansions that overrun established neighborhoods, even historic districts, with confused new purposes and expedient real-estate ventures.

For cities now in a damaged condition but still possessing continuity with past episodes in their history, it seems a decisive moment.

How much renovation a city might require probably depends upon how much of its life has, in C. F. Forester's term, "slipped into the grey." Currently a conflict exists in most industrial areas between what is permanent and what uses and expressions represent ephemeral social and economic purposes. Meaning and continuity might be more expressive in environments if activities intrinsic to a society's development were noticeably distinct from temporary demands.

The Problem of Connection

For many European cities this type of discrimination has been practiced for several centuries. London, Paris, Rome, for example, are capital cities which despite extensive renovations have maintained their historical settings. In these cities the human being enters many different environments exhibiting a movement through time and change. Transitional areas are usually well designed to protect the identity of each section without isolating it from the city's total composition. In large measure, this achievement can be attributed to the ability of architects, planners, and administrators to work together with ideas and procedures over long periods of time. Design concepts involving penetration into historic districts, or superimposing a new flow of

Concept of negative space

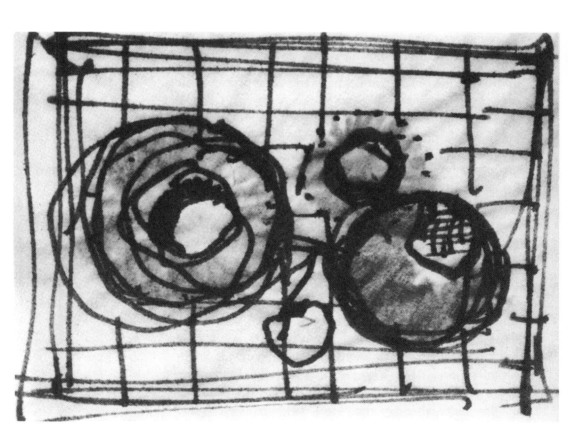

circulation into critical environments, have often resulted in interesting malls and axial avenues—lines
strong enough to carry with them a momentum ag-
grandizing their terminal points into great public
squares. These in turn provided magnificent settings for
sculpture and buildings.

Negative space, a neutral environment with latent
activity, also can be a useful design concept for societies which need to open up special environments for
the influx of new ideas and activities. Sometimes these
openings have become outlets for popular feelings.
For instance, St. Peter's Basilica, Buckingham Palace,
and the Kremlin are each surrounded by expansive
open space, which even when empty suggests their
ceremonial crowds. Negative spaces also can become
dramatic focal points, as in Paris where the Champs
Elysées, ending at the Arc de Triomphe, conveys historical scale and grandeur. Although some open spaces
in American cities, such as the Washington Monument,
recently have become symbolic meeting places for national demonstrations, they do not fulfill the more
subtle psychological—and certainly not the cultural—
function of a negative space.

On a larger scale the problem of connecting the
present with the past probably will remain critical for
the rest of this century and maybe longer, especially
for the recently independent nations of Africa, South
America, and Asia. Visually and socially, it appears
to be a dilemma of extremes. Uprooting all evidence
of the cultural past can lead to instability, while
propagating forms of expressions that no longer are

meaningful to the people may cause equally serious problems of identification.

Sketch for an American Forum

For this reason the concept of a forum acting as the people's voice seems to offer interesting possibilities. Although initially associated with Rome and its imperial ambitions, the forum image changed through Western history and now denotes democratic procedures.

The original direction of the American society, for example, was resolved in town meetings or forums. Could not the idea of a forum become pertinent again in this period of urban conflict and disintegration, to bring together factional groups and viewpoints?

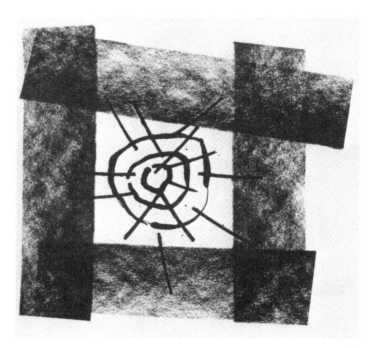

The forum, like an explosion, should pierce the monotony of cities and through its offshoots pump new life into the society

49

Today, without depriving its population of basic necessities, the United States can invest in a cultural life on a scale once inconceivable. Furthermore, conditions favor the formation of a total culture out of previously isolated elements. Community and regional forums could lead this movement by relieving tensions that strain individuals and groups in their struggle to retain their individuality, while seeking identification in a collective unity.

Because societies advance through the innovations and ideas of their creative people, the forum as a concept acts as a speaker amplifying the works of artists, artisans, scientists, and scholars. The image of

It might be necessary to carve the forum out of a city. The cavity would then become the new heart and draw the flow of life around it

a forum could indicate this civic role in its site planning and architecture. Just as organisms in nature balance their cores proportionately with their mass, so a forum should be designed to hold a pivotal role in society, to dominate not by its size but through its significance.

The image of this forum, with its many color patterns, openings, and rhythms, is derived from nature. In the sketch, the area above is a relaxation surface exposed to sunlight and landscape, which contrasts markedly with the darker and more intricate spaces below. Openings in the roof garden direct light and air into activity centers and retreats on lower levels. The ground floor, for instance, could be planned for public use and could provide facilities such as reading rooms, exhibition galleries, theaters, concert and lecture halls, music listening and practice rooms, and various visual studios for work in the arts and crafts.

Requirements for large public gatherings are located around the circumference, but the forum focuses upon individual activities that could occur in the center, and in this respect it is reminiscent of the acropolis image in Greek and Roman town planning.

More fundamentally, however, the forum is a concept of free space in a city and as shown in the model, it should be distinct from the character of its surroundings. Both its generic form and central setting suggest its imagery as a cultural bright spot attracting the flow of life around it.

Group Conflicts

As one of the recent nations to be composed of many racial and national minorities, the United States has struggled to include many cultural heritages and social patterns in the formation of its national image. Without

REVOLT

planning ahead, however, the society has met with chaos and anarchy in its cities. Their congested environments have become concentrations of conflict, confused random movements, and the intersection of hostile social forces. Crime, mental illnesses, and race riots have intensified. Under such tensions it is becoming evident that city structures cannot retain their past orders, nor satisfactorily establish new relationships.

Particularly ominous in the largest American cities are the explosive ghettos. With each increase in density or population mixture, conditions become so precarious that a change or accident can trigger spontaneous social violence. Police supervision does not change the psychological conditions disturbing these environments; in fact repressing latent social and racial clashes seems only to make them more volatile. Mercilessly, spots of misery act as continual sparks ready to ignite great social conflagrations. The potential violence in turn adds tensions to the daily life and upbringing of inhabitants.

52

When relationships and routines become distorted to such a degree that any increase of stress is apt to touch off a chain of reactions, the hostility underlying specific situations may demoralize an entire society, especially its structure of group relationships. Gang wars, race riots, and revolutionary uprisings demonstrate such webs of violence.

On an even greater scale of danger, the intersection of cultures menaces all levels of intergroup communication. Ironically, these cultural and racial collisions may be related directly to the breakdown of social barriers because, as well as being forms of oppression, these also have been protective shields. The concept of separation has been applied however in a discriminatory manner, and no longer is in scale with people's ability to move about the world. Other hypotheses are

The intersection of cultures

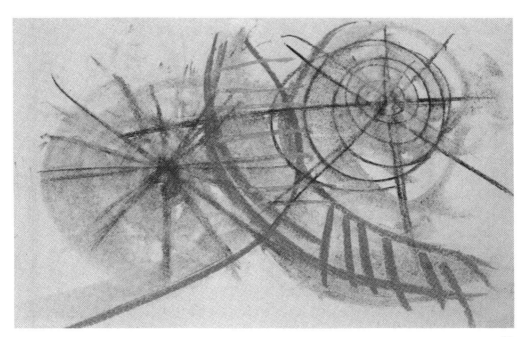

Forms of cultural protection

needed that can give contemporary solutions to the ancient problem of cultural protection.

The more difficult social and visual problem may be connection rather than separation, especially in societies encouraging environmental variation.

Superposition of living patterns

These counterparts—isolation and connection—might be visualized as social rhythms, expressible in community planning and architectural concepts. An integral design idea like superposition can become an organizing principle in hostile or isolated environments. Furthermore, the variegated structure suggests

The Belt as a Means of Connection

the excitement and continuity that is latent in the community life of a multiracial or multinational society.

A belt of civic activities uniting private and public parts of a city presents another design approach. A street on a much enlarged scale—a street on the scale of the whole city—is raised above the chaos of existing urban patterns. Symbolizing the communal life of all inhabitants and providing recreational and entertaining diversions, the belt is somewhat reminiscent of malls and public squares that opened up medieval cities.

The belt of connection, being a circular concept, ultimately simple and returning upon itself, unifies an urban landscape. Conveying a city's massive character, it could penetrate environments and express many occupations and interests. Not only historic and artistic monuments but vivid and anonymous scenes of people's lives would be viewable from perspectives on the belt. This kind of experience is described in Dostoyevsky's remark: "Commonplace people are at every moment the chief and essential links in human affairs; if we leave them out, we lose all semblance of truth" (*The Idiot*).

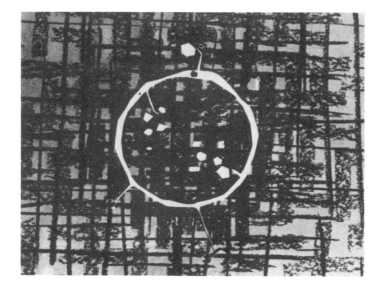

Through its offshoots, the belt can penetrate distinct areas and connect them with the mainstream of urban life

Offshoots from the ring can be thought about as lifelines reaching into isolated environments and releasing constrictions in a city's growth. Those intended

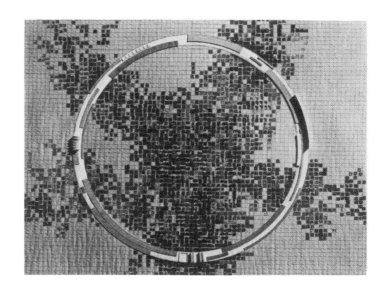

to be temporary could be designed to disappear as their purposes were accomplished. Other spurs, linking the belt activities with significant governmental and cultural settings, might develop into dramatic reference points in the urban landscape.

For variation in character and use the belt could change in dimension. Along a waterfront, for instance, it might widen to feature views and recreational environments. Passing through a commercial center, the belt could contract to provide only necessary pedestrian and vehicular accesses to shopping centers. Shopping and social services also could be included in the belt design.

Other changes in the belt's character might occur at residential contact points, designed as transitional environments to ease ethnic and racial frictions. The belt becomes a concept for joining together divergent social groups in a multiracial society, and for penetrating neighborhoods which are unhealthily ingrown.

Visualized as a function of leisure for an industrial society, the belt concept can offer the city dweller intervals of activities that contrast with work and home environments. Moreover, because of the considerable, and growing, proportion of free time in the industrial work week, the belt could be thought of as a stream of cultural and social diversions accessible to all sections, and to all inhabitants of the existing, inchoate city.

As a design concept the belt issues from the massive, overgrown city and introduces a communal scale and sequence to its aggregate environments.

CHAPTER 7

COMMUNAL FORMS

The city of power, dehumanized tribute to the stand-ardized industry of men and machines, nevertheless may fail—not owing principally to its size, nor to its labyrinthian complexity, and not because it does not tend to its inhabitants' business and governmental in-terests; but, more provocatively, because it has not taken account of their nonmaterial aspirations, es-pecially the elusive need for variety.

Variation: The Concept of Subsidiary Societies

It may become necessary for societies composed of such cities to sponsor subsidiary, and at times even divergent, communities within their frameworks. Some might be founded to further medical research or for other special concentrations of scientific work, or to foster distinct cultural and educational innovations. Even more interesting, there might be some experi-mental communities established to explore alternative courses of thought or to uphold values different from those offered by the general society. Visually and sociologically, the idea is one of discontinuity and pertains either to societies without cohesive cultures or to those seeking safeguards against total conformity. Considering the idea also in practical terms, the pro-posal to build entirely separate communities that can develop their own environmental characters may be less costly in both human and economic terms than try-ing to relate them to a society's typical, and possibly hostile, environments.

Subsidiary societies of this type certainly are not unprecedented in free societies. During the formative period of democracy in the United States, many religious and social sects like the Shakers, Mormons, Mennonites, as well as followers of Owen's economic idealism, built special communities.

Unfortunately, since they usually detached themselves from the society of their time, they failed to achieve their potential role in the American culture. Also, without public sanctions this type of social experimentation gradually perished but it seems intrinsic enough in the culture to persist in future communal innovations.

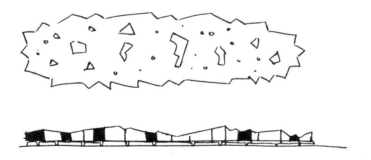

Communities can be conceived for special purposes. Their contrast with prevalent patterns could make them jewels of difference

The following sketches of subsidiary societies are speculations for either new or existing cultures. The emphasis is upon their conceptual and visual character. Furthermore, because each is considered to be an experience entire in itself, less attention has been given to surrounding areas.

The Monolith

A community might be the statement of people's lives, of their private and shared achievements and desires. Representing a gathering and interweaving of individuals, a composition of their activities, their living spaces, transportation routes, the places where they work, their art centers, educational institutes, their government and industries, a monolithic community also could be assumed to include all the thoughts and actions that it stimulates. Architecturally, the total intricate community could be rendered as one building, one container from which various towers spring out of lower complexes.

As an image, then, the monolith is a fusion of geometric and social form. Consider instances in the past which are similar: the pyramids of Egypt, the "cone" of Mont St. Michel.

The strong simplicity of the tombs rising abruptly from the sandy vastness of their landscape suggests the monolithic rule of the early Pharaohs. Again, the cone of St. Michel, its lower base pounded by thrashing waves, alludes to medieval concepts of man's life: his endless struggle for grace against overwhelming evil. Yet it is the upward thrust of its monolithic form which is so suggestive. The restlessness and striving of the Christian theology is reflected in the architecture soaring above the natural rock formations.

What about today's and tomorrow's monoliths? (One wonders if they will be research centers on the scale of Cape Kennedy or Los Alamos or the commercial networks of our towns and cities, or whether some large but idealistic undertaking will be their unifying purpose.) The dimensions of a monolith might be several miles in either direction, depending upon the proposed density and estimated population. Vehicular

61

circulation as well as service functions would be aspects of a general circulation design that could penetrate the spaces and volumes of the monolith. For instance, there might be crossovers between towers as well as tunnels below ground and connections at grade level. Accordingly, circulation design on all levels would fashion a horizontal and vertical network.

Visually the towers and crossovers would give an uplift, a sense of activity above. Helicopters could land on the tower roofs so that there would be upper as well as lower exits from the city. Designating access points and hubs of activity as much above as at ground level or underground would tend to change upward and downward connotations and perhaps even reorient associations of gravity. Such conjectures of a monolith also allude to experiences in man-made satellites.

In essence, the monolith is an integral idea proposing to raise a community above its daily routines and envision its totality. Looking out from high levels of its network, one can imagine seeing the natural landscape of a surrounding countryside continue to the

The monolith

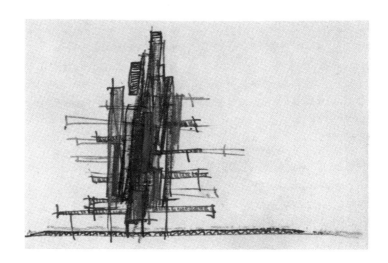

edges of a monolith without meeting the usual impedance of blighted areas. To reinforce the strong monolithic image and to prevent compromise by intrusions from adjacent regional developments, expanses of water might be used in a manner similar (although on a much larger scale) to the lakes and moats surrounding Renaissance chateaus to reflect the sculptural nature, the compelling order and wholeness of the monolithic concept.

**Growth Rings;
An Evolutionary
Community**

Architecturally, a city of rings might express the character of a "natural" society—in particular its ease and order of change—while remaining a consistent and complete design idea. Absolute and even austere as the image may appear to be, it is basic to the notion of a "natural" community that design solutions take into account fluctuating functions and needs. Therefore, it would be wrong in this context to impose any code or custom upon the communal life. Clearly this interpretation of the term "nature" includes more than land-

scapes; its imagery suggests the total physical environment in which a person behaves, thinks, feels, and so on. A city of rings, then, is a serene and extremely pure representation of a human society.

The organization of community life could evolve physically as well as culturally out of the reasoning and psychic processes of the people. This design idea expresses the thought that the direction of human life is toward self-realization.

Indeed the visual and social imagery are so integral in the design concept of the growth rings that human functions could be assumed to be always in proper scale and balance with respect to each other and the community's total frame of reference. Change, even explosive expansion, is not foreseen to be disruptive because it is anticipated in the organic design of the growth rings.

PART III

ARCHITECTURE BEYOND CITIES

"Under existing conditions latecomers have the singular advantage of benefiting from the experiences and accomplishments of older nations."

(Awo: *The Autobiography of Chief Obafemi Awolowo*)

CHAPTER 8

MASS MOVEMENT AND HESITATIONS

Regardless of the type of government structure, world societies have become increasingly dependent upon popular endorsement. Therefore, techniques which demonstrate the thinking, wants, and purposes of the masses are now components of political power. Algeria, Cuba, and Vietnam show how the collective will of native populations has been wielded effectively enough to gain their goal of national independence. Unfortunately demagoguery and mobocracy also loom as likely mass-scale movements in societies that fail to work creatively with the force of men in number.

Mass-scale movement is a visual means of communication, as student groups have been demonstrating to the world. Even before these confrontations, however, the civil-rights marches by Martin Luther King proved to be effective mass-scale movements. A study of mass movement in society is imaginable, then, in terms of human forces that direct and are engendered by a culture.

It seems probable not only that past environments will be disrupted, even eradicated, by enormous changes in scale and demands for space, but also that uncontrolled conditions could make all surroundings insufferable. The population "explosion" which now threatens most continents is one ominous example. These coming

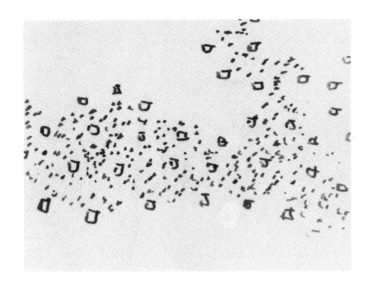

problems call attention to the obvious need for clear and inclusive designs of circulation, especially in environments designed for mass-scale use. For example, walking from intimate, intensely individuated activities and their alignment along streets into the openness and random movement of a public open space describes an enjoyable experience which is associated with Europe's older cultural centers. When changes of scale and movement are not stated boldly enough, however, monotony and psychological depression become the strongest environmental experience. In contrast with too little spatial definition in environments is the other extreme of confinement, of movement becoming too restricted. Claustrophobic fears then can be aroused. This type of insensitivity in the handling of people and the spaces serving their needs is now so typical in urban environments that it becomes more

**The Scale of
Mass Movement**

and more important to interpret mass movement in corresponding spatial and psychological terms.

In applying these thoughts to contemporary mass societies, the customs and symbols of restraint that underlie the government structures of Europe and North America, and which have evolved through historic struggles between the Individual and the State, no longer seem to apply. Today's image is not the focal point or authority, the patriarchal palace or church, but the rhythmic repetitions of city blocks, mass produced goods, and mass-scale needs.

Circulation may be delineated, for example, as a succession of spatial rhythms. Conceived of as visual elements opening up the urban landscape, their scale, detail, and spatial positions could be planned so that they would allay fears and potential panic in crowds. At critical points of circulation they could become deflectors preventing stagnation in the movement of

*A succession of
spatial rhythms*

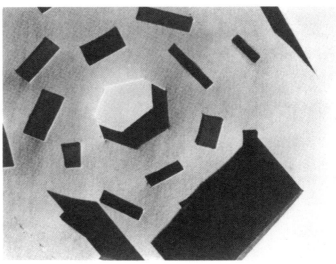

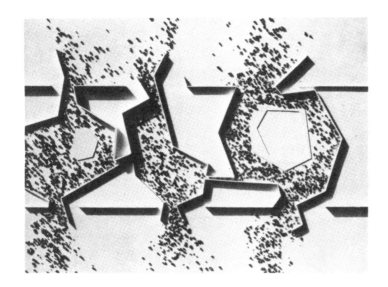

Spaces in a self-governing society designed for mass movement

crowds and the even greater danger of an ensuing swarming motion.

Deflecting forms can instigate a varied yet controlled movement in environments, the intention being to guide people in large numbers without coercing them. Furthermore, because mass movement can mesmerize individuals in threatening numbers, government leaders, planners, and architects may wish to work symbolically with latent cultural forms. These might be assumed to vary from traditions underlying a society's stability and cultural morale to a people's unconscious dissatisfactions and desires. Many new nations in Africa, for example, are seeking social substitutes for the tribal organization which the national structure is displacing.

Working with the scale of mass movement can become a highly abstract and sculptural undertaking. The stairways, malls, and galleries of the palace and gardens at Versailles suggest magnificently the movement of a royal court. When one realizes that the association between physical movement and musical harmony was understood and used by Mansart at the time of their construction, the example becomes even more interesting. Eisenstein's portrayals of the behavior of crowds, in films such as *Potemkin*, are even more applicable to future studies of mass movement. What these examples signify is that spaces and circulation patterns express a society's life patterns and type of leadership. Thus, the Lion's Gate at Mycenae, or the Forum in Rome, or the Red Square in Moscow, may be regarded as mass-scale imagery.

Mass-scale movement

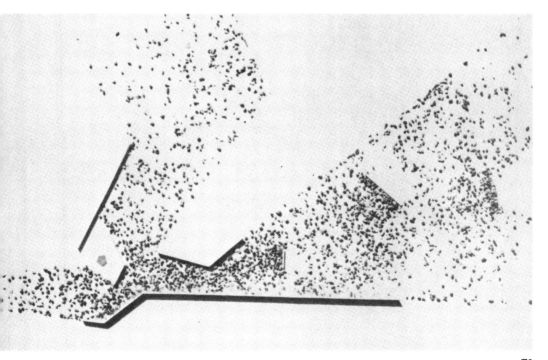

How might cultural forms be used to help solve the dilemma: without order there can be no peace—only flux, chaos; but without freedom there cannot be growth, novelty, change, experimentation, chance for creative mutations? Particularly for societies controlled by mass movements, those processes which give power to the part with respect to the whole—decentralization, individuation—seem likely to become essential to their stable functioning.

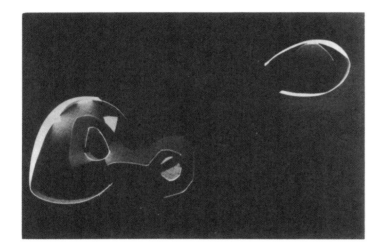

It appears likely also that inhibitions and incentives will be engineered into group behavior, especially if as collective motivations they could persist long enough to become archetypes. As such, they would be effective not only as a code of ethics but visually as symbolic forms

Movement, like technology, is an existential fact of life for both individuals and groups in contemporary societies. Therefore, why not visualize the contrasting human scales—one relating to man in singular terms, the other to men in their plurality—as interacting variables? Why not represent individual movement in society as abstractly as mass movements and work with it as a corresponding social rhythm?

Free Action and Collective Movement in Society

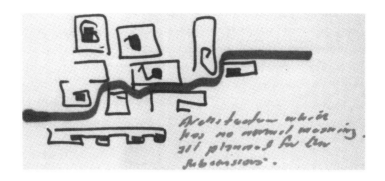

A family can be imagined as a nucleus of movement within a residential community. Through the family, one initially becomes involved with society. One moves in its physical and psychological surroundings. In more general terms, individual relationships might be thought of as determining the size and character of environments whose participants—including both those who are members of family units and others who have selected other bonds of relationship—move at random, self-driven by the free forces of inner development, interests, and singular abilities.

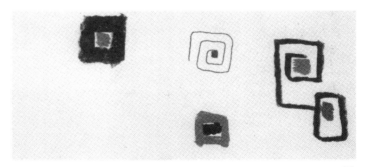

Best suggested in an imagery of movement, hesitations (as one might term the clusters of activity) compose an individual's private life in society. Envisioned as evolutionary ideas, they become episodes of eating, sleeping, working, relaxing, learning, within a stream of time and space. Some living functions are essentially open and may be shared with a number of people, while others are by nature solitary.

One can express the change in intensity from open to closed functions, from continuous to isolated activity, as movement and hesitation.

The spatial continuity between environmental functions implies that one would be absolutely free to develop a scope and sequence of activities by the day, lifetime, year—the increments of time, like the uses of space, being individual determinations. Consequently, neither spaces nor the functions which they accommodate are indicated by conventional social or visual imagery, but as episodes, stops, integrals of enclosed, inclusive movement.

Hesitations

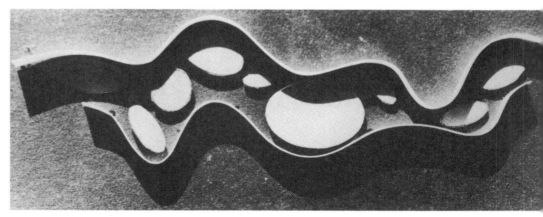

*Free movement
within a limited
environment*

Conceivably, the totality of human energies which alternately are stimulated by and expended upon functions of a particular social environment could be visualized. A community engaged in farming operations would show its distinctness from one involved with research or education—whose functions and form in turn would not develop like those in commercial or governmental environments. Each human settlement, then, could indicate a unique social and visual character, an identity not externally imposed but intrinsic to its life commitments.

Rather than assume, then, that individual and collective roles in society are separate involvements, one can suppose them issuing from an inclusive life context. Accordingly one might visualize an environment such as a "total living space" and work abstractly with its changing spatial rhythms and expanding scales of social relationship.

Probing further, why not abandon limits altogether in order to create environments which are porous both to the free pursuits of individuals and to strong collective movements? Although untested, the hypothesis seems to be revealing, particularly when one is puzzled by how closely the different scales of needs are paired: the desire for direction in mass movement related to the individual's sense of purpose; the importance of reference points in mass-scale movement with securing, relating the self to the world outside; and the mass appetite for variety implying individual free will.

The Idea of a "Total Living Space"

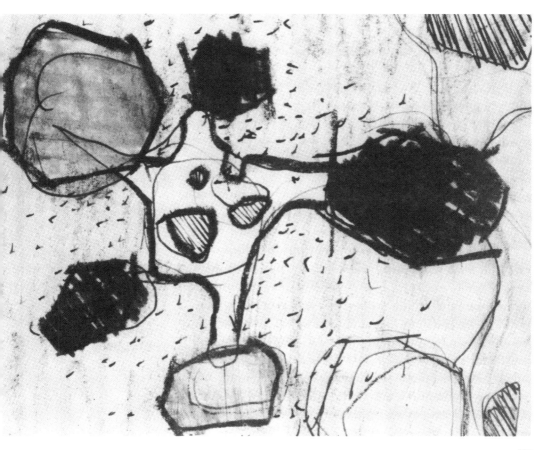

CHAPTER 9

THE CONSTRUCTION OF NEW SOCIETIES

Societies now embarking upon mass programs of physical and social welfare presumably will arrive in due course at a total evolutionary order. Predictably, too, they will encounter new design scales and purposes.

For this reason, evaluating the construction of societies from the viewpoint of their capacity to solve problems of ever-increasing magnitude and contingency without distorting their generic forms becomes more and more relevant, especially if much of the brutality that characterized the initial stages of the Chinese and Russian development programs is to be prevented in future instances. With such an approach, a society's planned development would be required to give priority to human well-being at all stages.

Consequently design and planning proposals need to be examined not only in present but in future contexts. Options appearing momentarily desirable to a society while obstructing its inherent growth patterns and permanent values—either through promoting confusion or by resisting the drift of original customs and thoughts—would be apt to show up plainly in visual and social studies that project decisions into successive stages of materialization. Through such screening and modeling mechanisms, critical errors that now seem unavoidable in long-range planning should become detectable.

New Design
Scales and
Purposes

Superimposing an order upon life's pulsations

What will characterize these new approaches to physical and social planning, and what will be the scope of architecture beyond cities?

It is time to consider the structure of societies from the standpoint of their generic forms. For instance, linear patterns suggest large, accessible, and expansive continents; while focal cities tend to evolve in populous surroundings which may also be, like parts of Europe, geographically and culturally localized. Another prototype, the island development, produced the Cretan, British, Japanese, Greek, and Polynesian civilizations.

Recognizing that every human society conforms to characteristics of its type, contemporary and future societies can consciously use such forms to guide their self-determined evolutions.

Relating national government structures and planning policies to these generic forms is creative work. Hypothetically, one can imagine that even the obvious benefits gained from balancing the allocation and development of essential resources could be more than offset by eroding social conditions—those conflicts and weaknesses that undermine a society because it has chosen an ill-fitting prototype. For instance, for a society geographically limited in size and concentrated in population to apply planning procedures originating from a large, diverse, continental society could be coercive as well as self-defeating.

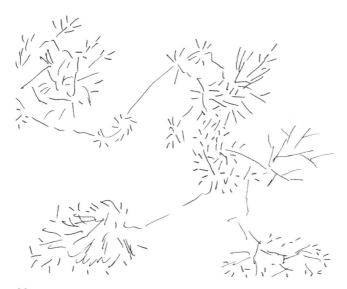

Societies as Configurations

Turning attention to an existing design condition, some cultural formations seem to be producing configurations of focal points. Urban concentrations in the United States are sending out tentacles—communication and transportation arteries that connect with other centers. As might have been foreseen, the landscape has been penetrated—spewn with settlements—by the character and force of these nodal points.

Conceivably, however, transitional environments could become primary means of coping with society's growth, of expressing the process of its social and physical self-realization. Working farsightedly with this concept as a design approach, cities could release selected spurs—visualized as pulsations—from their most intense points of generation. Initially these outbursts of energy might produce sporadic expansions, but ultimately their function is to join disparate parts into a consummate previewed order.

Traveling from focus to focus in such a culture could become an exciting diversion available on a mass scale to an entire population. However, unlike cities along the Eastern seaboard of the United States where the same patterns are repeated, the same densities are tolerated, and the same values predominate, the focal points would be designed and controlled to protect variety, local privacy, independence, and especially authenticity. If such excursions were contemplated on mass scale, for like traveling down the Nile with side trips to the great monuments of Egypt, the repercussions upon transportation media, and recreational and conservation resources, could become significant design and planning responsibilities for a national agency. The sequence of experiences might

recall, although on a much larger scale, the movement through a city and the enjoyment of exploring its changes of environment.

Foreseeably, island formations are the most suitable prototypes to develop interesting configurations. Because they are generally networks of separate units, collisions between strong focal centers are unlikely. A typical example, islands in the Caribbean have populations that differ in race, nationality, language, social customs, and cultural inheritance. Although this variation happened accidentally from the way that the islands were colonized by European powers, each ethnic and national grouping has continued—no doubt helped in a Darwinian sense by being separated by water—to conform to its initial cultural framework even after the foreign domination was removed.

Turning this example into a design approach, components in a configuration, besides each being a generic force and unity in itself, also would become integrals, parts in a sequence of designed movement.

Either from expansion pressures or for special cultural and social purposes, island configurations also may become in the future useful adjuncts to existing continental societies. One can visualize islands being constructed off the East Coast of the United States to serve as recreational areas for the dense urban belt of industrial cities. While some islands might be developed actively as resorts, others could become places agreeable for contemplation—retreats or research cen-

Island forms

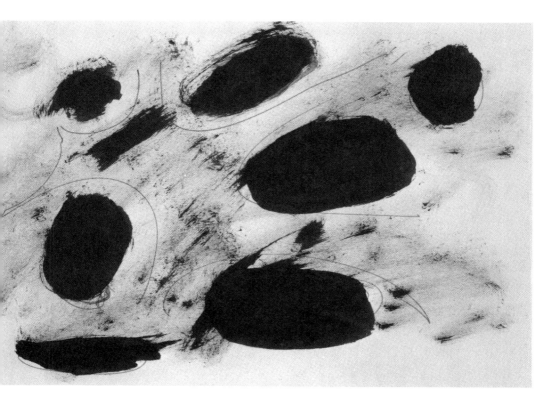

ters which have access to, but also privacy from, cluttered and diverse mainland centers.

Islands could be developed abstractly as fantasies. A more distant future possibility is the construction of satellite islands on nearby planets or as orbiting entities in space. Perhaps some of the visual and social concepts solutions that are experimented with in present island cultures will be creative enough to apply to the formation of human environments on these unexplored and vaster scales.

CHAPTER 10

DESIGN OF A LINEAR SOCIETY

Unlike previous civilizations whose ideals and procedures seem in retrospect to have been relatively stable and predictable, societies today and in the future can initiate new living conditions and exploit their resources at such rates that the urgency to design for growth and mobility appears obvious. In fact, seen from a later perspective, developing skills that control these forces may be critical for survival.

The evolution of growth lines becomes a design of motion

The linear society and other environmental concepts discussed in this book represent planned yet noncoercive approaches to a society's self-developments. As evolutionary ideas they are especially appropriate to the conditions of new twentieth-century societies. For this reason they are presented abstractly as a framework to be improvised upon—completed by—the existential situation.

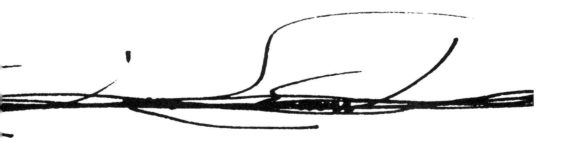

Despite awareness of the need for inclusive planning among those involved with today's populous and industrial societies, strong, simple, and complete concepts are often criticized out of concern for variation in a society. Variety is not discernible, however, without simplicity, without a clear framework against which it can be appreciated. At the present time in industrial societies the need for variety has been answered by waste and clutter.

Seen in this context the linear society is an imagined response to insolvable entanglements, to the overgrowth of forms—in fact to all the abrasive juxtapositions in environments of the American and similar societies that wear away life's well-being. In these terms the city no longer remains an isolated social or visual form. Just the opposite; the proposal is involved with the organization of a whole society or aggregate of nations, even with relating nations of dissimilar frameworks. Articulating changes of activity, scale, and topography—actually the inclusive life patterns—of rural regions and urban concentrations is its proper design concern.

Indeed through the grayness, the monotonous deterioration and anonymity of industrial centers can be seen the simple, balanced structure of a linear society. One traces too its intrinsic planning—its clear, consistent rationality—which recognizes that each of a society's major functions can be accorded its essential needs, and that paramount among these are the pressures of expansion. Treating them from the beginning as potential forms that should be included in present as well as future design decisions seems especially valuable to societies in their embryonic stages.

To relegate a society's principle development to

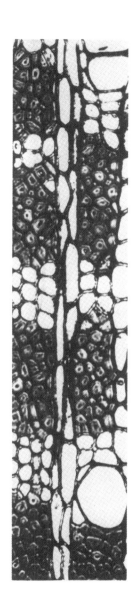

Evolution of growth lines in the organic world

separate growth lines means initiating a movement, a direction, that becomes difficult to counteract or subvert. One might speculate also upon several likely social repercussions. Decay, disorder, and conflict do not seem as predictable in environments of such visual clarity. One can imagine feeling an ease, a pleasure, from understanding the relationship between activities as one moves through the distinct, expressive environments evolving on the different growth lines.

Although the design idea of a linear society was intuitive—its image seen as an abstract framework underlying, attracting, on occasion even fusing with the spontaneous vivid impulses of everyday life—it has become increasingly apparent over the past few decades of population explosion that this form of social organization is not at all imaginary but a very real and visible pattern of human settlement. This linear movement has become a wave of development moving along the densely populated eastern and western coastlines of the United States, but it may be even more obvious along the western Mediterranean.

Taking the thirty-kilometer stretch between Cannes and Nice as a specific example, one notes that this linear movement consists of several belts of activity which run parallel to each other and to the seacoast, bending where it bends, hollowing out into harbors, concentrating into cities, but always continuous. The cross section of this linear development is also strongly and visibly defined. Along one edge runs a six-story wall of apartments and hotels two or three blocks in depth, while on its other boundary the linear form opens to the Mediterranean Sea. In between run distinct lines of activity that are separated from each other by differences in use and in speed. Whether

87

walking or driving, one is definitely aware of these parallel belts of activity, and aware that their movement is broken only at intervals for cross circulation and changes in direction.

Looking toward the sea from the longostrada, one sees that the linear rhythms of restaurants, bathhouses, and beach umbrellas denote activity and movement more intimate in scale and less directional than those of vehicles and crowds on adjacent belts.

The linear pattern of settlement along the French and Italian Riviera came about by chance. It demonstrates however that the linear form is capable of coping with expansion pressures produced by advanced industrial societies and can absorb their urban scales and densities in an orderly and human way. Also, we found corroboration for our conjecture that growth lines do not terminate naturally at national borders, but are inherently supranational. Generated by the collective energies of the Mediterranean peoples, these growth streams can be seen in all their geographical and cultural variety, their changes in intensity and local character, as they have expanded from center to cen-

Growth lines

ter and have connected the entire coastline from St. Tropez to La Spezia. What this linear movement has initiated is an organization of society which applies to the prototype design study that follows.

The Concept of Growth Lines

The simplest instance to imagine of a nation recomposing itself and designating its principle private and public development along growth lines of a linear society would be one which had not yet assumed the norms of modern urban life. Regardless of its status today, such a society holds an overwhelming advantage if its organizational framework avoids the confusion and tragic conflicts that are eroding the world's most powerful societies. The total yet evolutionary order of the growth lines therefore seems particularly suitable for societies whose social, economic, political, and cultural processes are emerging out of the stagnation and chaos of foreign domination.

At first lines in space, growth streams of a society can become three dimensional through the historical process. Geography too would influence their definition. Over mountainous terrain or water, for instance, the linear form might almost disappear; and in some

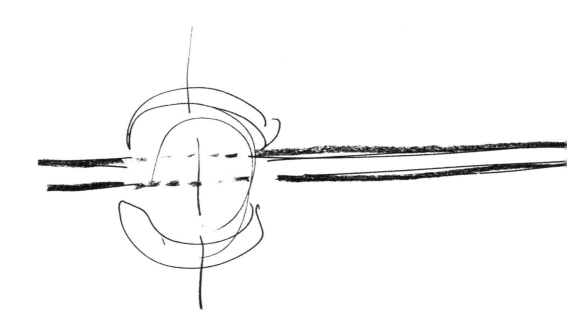

regions which were not yet developed, the growth lines could be treated simply as a government right of way. Yet as latent forms, they still would shape future surges of activity.

There seems good reason to incorporate important thoroughfares (air routes as well as those over land or by water) into the overall design of the growth lines to spur the opening up of new territories. Already African and Asian spokesmen have noted the significance of this kind of approach. The design implications, however, extend further. They indicate how an entire society might be planned with the result that "remote areas" no longer would exist. The growth lines become a frame of reference giving position—relationship and locus—to all points within their limits.

One perceives inhabitants of such a society becoming visually oriented so that in time they see the ab-

stract patterns created by their daily associations, and as a result develop environments sensitive to the tempo of movement and constantly changing scales of social relationship.

Subdivisions of Growth Lines

How a society choosing a linear form of development would subdivide its basic functions into growth lines probably would depend upon the structure of relationships that were revealed in the work, living, and leisure habits of the people more than on its government structure and the extent of its centralized control. Societies committed to private or to communal ownership of property could equally well develop the characteristics of a linear society, although the potentialities for richer social interactions probably are greatest under a system of collective ownership.

The sample linear society which is illustrated in abstract terms assumes an industrialized economy; it also assumes that a high level of technical inventiveness has been achieved. These qualifications are thought of as the norms of the twentieth century, whether or not they have been achieved by all societies in the world at present.

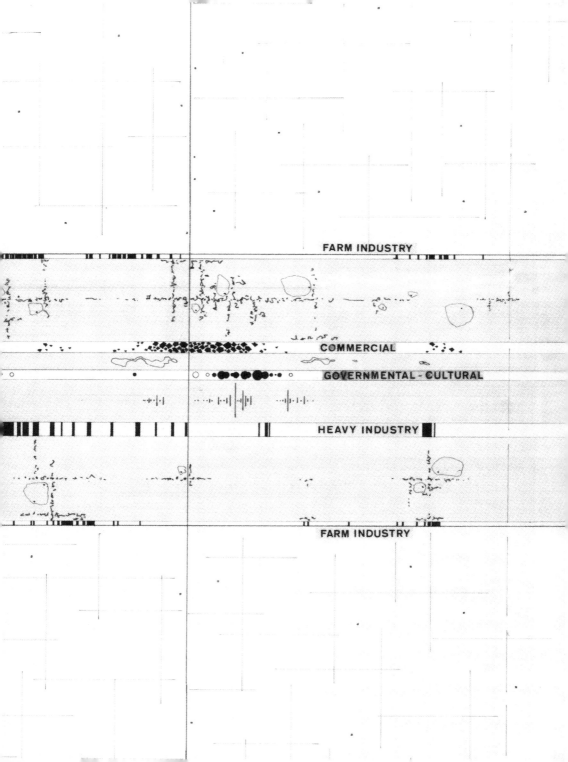

FARM INDUSTRY

COMMERCIAL

GOVERNMENTAL - CULTURAL

HEAVY INDUSTRY

FARM INDUSTRY

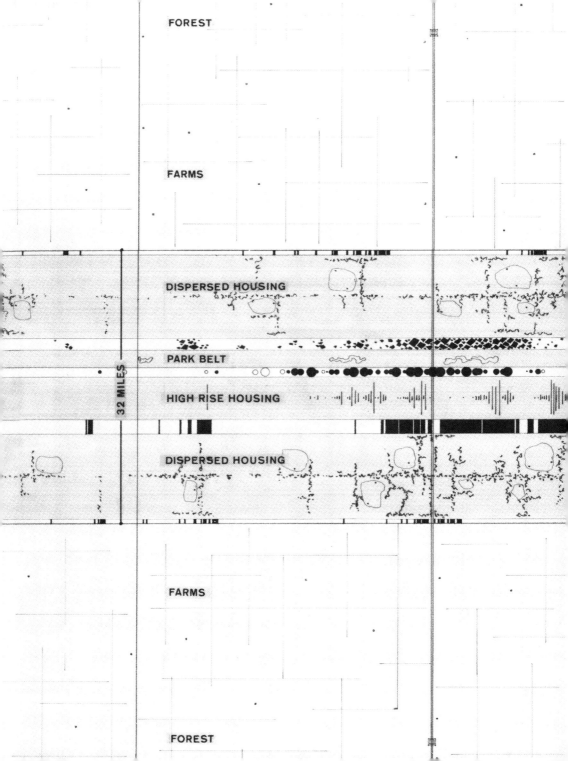

FOREST

FARMS

DISPERSED HOUSING

PARK BELT

HIGH RISE HOUSING

DISPERSED HOUSING

FARMS

FOREST

32 MILES

In this prototypal plan the governmental, educational, commercial, and industrial functions, including their related residential developments, are shown subdivided into parallel growth lines. The forest and farm belts are the largest and least densely settled. Very different from their patterns are the concentrations of activity and the intense rhythms which signify the heavy industry, commercial, and government-cultural belts. Parks and several types of residential areas are indicated as interim strips between these major growth lines. One can see, for example, that a high-rise type of residential development is located between the heavy industry and government-cultural belts because it seemed reasonable to suppose that there would be a maximum concentration of people involved in both centralized activities. In contrast, dispersed housing is shown related to large farming and forest tracts, and two concepts of low-rise housing are suggested for the residential belt adjacent to the growth lines for commercial functions and light industry.

Although in this prototype study of a linear society the growth lines are dimensioned and the total cross section of the linear society (including its farm and forest zones) scales two hundred miles, in actual circumstances the width of each belt would be determined by a society's physical size and resources. However, the cross section is thought of as being always a dimension that could be comprehended easily by persons living and working in any environment included within it. One imagines being able to see from belt to belt.

It might be desirable, then, to think of changes in tempo along the parallel growth lines—the high-key tensions and pressures of urban densities followed by the steadiness of life in more sparsely settled sections —as being spatial experiences that are somewhat analogous to musical pulsations. Also, like musical counterpoint, the rhythm of life on each belt could be designed intentionally to correspond with, or to offset, the intensity of adjacent growth lines.

Comments on the General Circulation

Abstractly, the circulation in a linear society might be thought about as generating two opposite directions of movement. One, the longitudinal, would be fast, unobstructed. The other, a transversal flow, is expressed as a filtering movement representing the free, self-willed actions of individuals. The design of circulation along and across the belts would influence the character of environments, both those that might be termed most typical in a linear society because of their identification with its predominant longitudinal movement, and others which through their involvement with functions on several belts would properly express its filtering or transversal movement.

A design of circulation

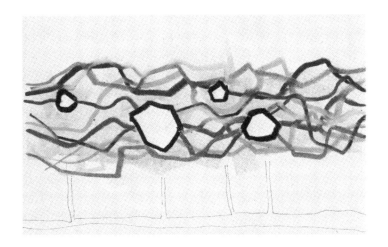

Circulation patterns should adjust to environmental conditions. In concept, they are considered to be flexible lines in space rather than the traffic routes of today

The ways that people move about, either on foot or by vehicle, should be designed to be a pleasant as well as efficient means of circulation. Through changes of scale and character circulation designs should help to connect the natural and given environments with those that men construct. For instance, walkways on the commercial belt might be multilevel on occasion to bypass intense activity—the energies of a people "getting and spending"—and the malls indicated on the government-cultural growth line could be meditative, closely related to nature.

Lookout platforms accentuate the architectural concepts of movement along the growth lines

From a design viewpoint, the approaches to environments on the growth lines are of great significance because they offer an opportunity to introduce a new kind of experience into the planning and architecture of public buildings. As openings and connecting links, they change the character of surroundings entirely from the self-contained and static monumentality of the past's great focal points.

The Study of Architecture Along the Growth Lines

Although there would be many influences—some of the more obvious being climate, topography, traditional and available building materials, and methods of construction—upon the architecture of a linear society, perhaps the most important ones to consider now are those generic to its design concept. For example, what are some of the foreseeable effects upon planning and architectural procedures from the prominence in a linear society of the silhouette or profile view of build-

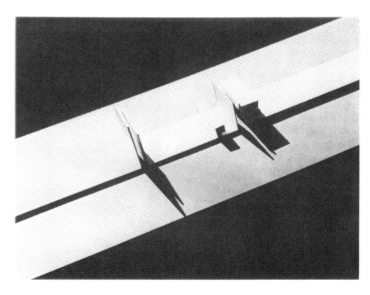

Architectural profile of a belt

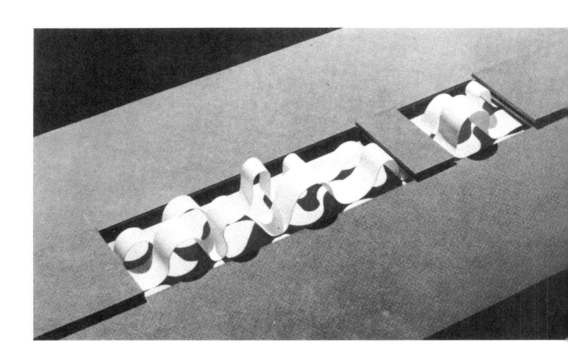

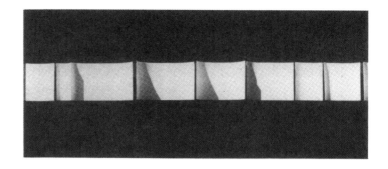

ings? One thinks especially of the design possibilities along the edges of the growth lines because these could be seen in elevation from adjacent belts. The profile view would then become an impressive feature in the design of a total landscape.

One likely metaphor for the architecture of the growth lines is a wave motion that would billow into a towering verticality in some locations and then smooth out where social, cultural, and industrial ac-

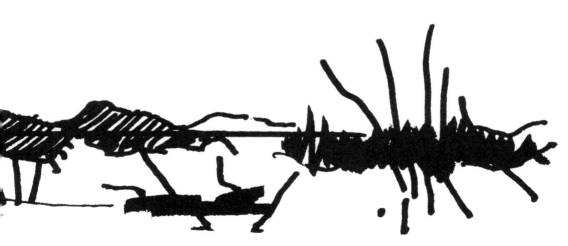

tivities were less concentrated. Abstractly, development might be visualized as a ribbon rising above and penetrating below the ground plane, its thrust of expansion impeded at intervals by difficult topographical conditions in some regions but regaining momentum further along a growth line and surging to new peaks of activity.

The relative development of the growth lines should be expected to vary according to a region's resources and productivity. Industrial functions would be apt to precede others in opening up a new territory if cultural and educational institutions are expected to rely upon their economic support. This kind of sequence would be reflected, of course, in a linear society. Instead of presuming that its growth lines would produce a uniform development at any cross section, it seems truer to picture them as being parallel and intricately balanced movements determining the expansion of the whole society.

Governmental educational, and cultural functions (in this example the lifeline of a linear society) are centrally located as shown on the prototype plan. The

Government-Cultural Growth Line

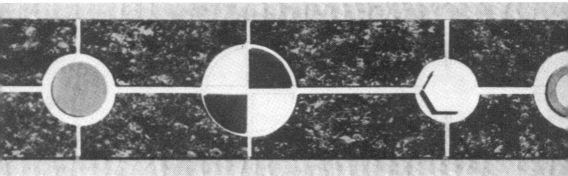

proposed width of the belt is approximately one mile, the dimension suggesting that its environments could accommodate either one or several simultaneous activities at any cross section.

An environment designed to be a sequence of experiences

An interesting architectural idea, one that is a ramification of the society's generic concept, is an environment generated as a series by activity centers and the designed flow of people and communication between them. In this sketch a dominant axial artery penetrates successive cores and strongly states the connection between them, while the buffer zones shown surrounding each center suggest that separation is as basic a design idea as connection to an environmental series. Its scale and architectural character could indicate that none of the environmental centers are intended to be complete in themselves, but are meant to be experienced as a sequence of visual and social movement.

Presuming a minimum of commercial activity on the government-cultural growth line, its environments could become reflections—as honest as possible—of the society's basic framework. Symmetry is an appropriate imagery for this symbolism, as is indicated in this

sketch in which a long axial avenue approaches an important public function from both directions and is intended to accentuate its relevance to the society. The immediate surroundings are understated for the aesthetic reason of intensifying the contrast between them and the central activity. A government capitol or advanced educational institution are the kinds of use warranting such social and visual emphasis.

Applicable to a university or research center in which each department or project can be treated as an independent although integral unit, the modular concept suggests repetitive functions like classrooms and research laboratories. The architectural regularity of the identical units expresses an environmental neutrality. It questions applying the concept of monumentality to all public buildings. An understatement of forms

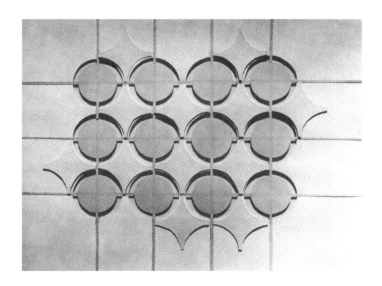

places attention on the people and the work that they are doing.

The lower platforms surrounding the cylinders could be used for administrative and public functions like adult education programs, art exhibitions, and large meeting spaces (theaters, auditoriums, and lecture halls). Some of these activities should be involved with social rehabilitation because all processes of regenera-

tion are the inherent imagery of the government-cultural growth line.

This growth line, concerned with the changing economic needs of a society's public and private development, has a vibrating character. Ranging from banking and other financial operations connected with government and industry to the innumerable private buying and selling transactions of people in their daily lives, the belt would vary from an inward orientation upon its own activities to an outward movement to other growth lines.

An example of these contrasting commercial relationships is shown in the design of a filtering movement, primarily in the longitudinal direction. Although there are many openings toward adjacent belts, the main circulation route is along a central mall. Those environments designed for a meandering, partly enclosed type of pedestrian circulation could be developed into shopping centers. Passageways from the mall lead into subsidiary areas, of which some might be

Commercial Belt

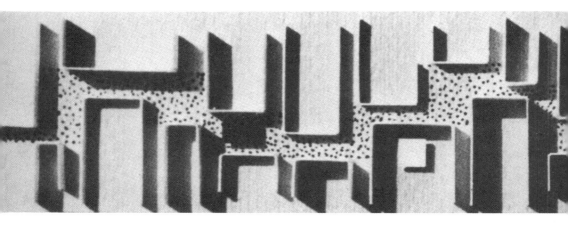

for professional offices, others for general health functions, including medical clinics, diagnostic and immunization centers. Ideally the controlled yet informally organized pattern of movement expresses the free character of individual pursuits within the framework of a publicly organized linear society.

Movement on the commercial belt also can be generated in a transversal direction. This sketch of a filtering action shows how commercial functions could connect with other belts at particular points. Random circulation patterns cater to the impulse-buying habits of consumers and might develop the spirit of "casbahs."

At nodal points where the commercial belt is intersected by important transversal arteries from other growth lines, an exchange point for goods and services would be apt to develop. Other nations could be represented at these trading points making available local, national, and world markets for product interchange.

Besides buying and selling transactions, the constant contacts between people who influence national policy and rates of growth and the financial supervision of

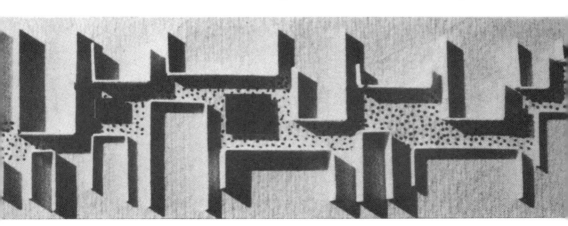

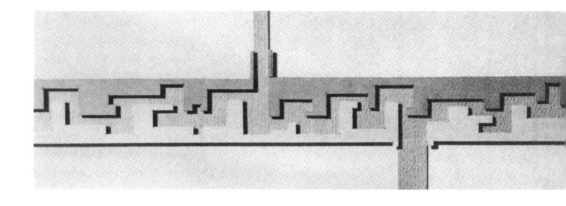

multistaged development programs make these commercial contact points important nerve centers of the whole linear society.

A modern society makes its major investment in developing its natural resources and expanding its industrial power as rapidly and efficiently as possible. Consequently on the industrial-growth line of this linear society, large-scale manufacturing operations (steel mills, factories making heavy machinery, transportation vehicles, perhaps shipbuilding, mass-produced housing and schools, as well as consumer appliances) are indicated as development lines that would continue in response to national demands for expansion and innovation.

Heavy Industry

The scope of the heavy industrial functions is such that regional differences and opportunities would probably characterize some manufacturing processes. Shipbuilding, as an example, may be supposed to occur only where good port facilities exist; steel mills, forging and smelting operations at present depend upon available power sources and access to raw materials. With the likelihood, however, that nuclear energy will become a common source of power, the location of industries need not be planned in the future according to conditions governing the older, established industrial societies. A linear type of industrial development, then, would be very feasible, since it can accommodate production processes, especially their needs for flexible expansion, more naturally than the industrial concentrations that now surround metropolitan areas.

Industrial processes are of such magnitudes in scale and equipment and investment—and are also so critically involved with all other functions of a society—that they are visualized in this prototype design as being publicly owned and controlled. The industrial environment can be a simple statement of the work accomplished in its areas with the design emphasis upon cooperation and continuity.

Manufacturing processes are shown in this sketch to be inwardly oriented. Driven by machine speeds and production schedules, striving for greater efficiencies, industrial processes can be penetrated by other values only at their entrance and exit points. To help compensate for tensions and human monotony that are inherent in assembly-line operations, very different environments should be available to workers during their leisure time.

Recreational and leisure facilities should be planned in the factory layout to be accessible to people in all jobs. During free periods in their working day, these centers could offer a variety of activities, including additional training courses, so that workers could choose to study, relax, or exercise. Circulation is direct and would be mainly in the longitudinal direction with rail and truck routes running along the edges of the belt. The supply and transfer of goods and raw materials to other manufacturing districts on the belt would be handled on these transportation arteries. Observational circulation, although of minimal functional importance, might be provided purely as an interesting environmental experience. When traveling along the belt longitudinally, one would be exposed directly to the scale and character of different industrial operations carried on by the society. For youth-training programs, this observational circulation might be important educationally, and it also would be an effective way to demonstrate the society's development to foreign visitors.

Although the architecture shows a modular, large-scale, and utilitarian character, the profile view of the industrial belt would be visible to adjacent residential areas. Color, texture, and penetrations in the continuous wall elevation might be treated abstractly as views to be enjoyed from those vistas.

Responding to growth pressures on any belts of a linear society, high-rise housing could be developed in residential areas to prevent a housing shortage from occurring at any cross section. For example, it could be expected that industrial workers would shift jobs frequently and therefore not live in one dwelling place

High-Rise Residential Living Units

long enough to warrant the unique architectural expression of a single-family house. High-rise residential units also pertain to the government-cultural growth line, where again a high turnover of personnel could be assumed in all types of jobs. Furthermore, if such high-rise housing developments made it possible to accommodate easily a constant influx of people from all regions of a society, even from other nations, coming to perform special tasks for brief intervals, the society would be encouraging a dedication to public service from its own members and also would gain outside help and stimulation from foreign cultures. In social terms of personal responsibility and unselfishness this type of activity might resemble the religious practice of tithing.

Residential flexibility is indicated in the sketch-model by the varying heights and spacing of the buildings, the design idea being that random changes in density are inherent in the planning and architectural framework. A central tube of services connects the high-rise units. It is generally above ground level in order to permit an open circulation (particularly by vehicles) through and around the buildings themselves. People living in the apartment units would have direct access to this line of community services as it intersected and passed through their building.

Adjacent to the heavy-industry and farm-industry belts, areas of dispersed housing could be developed. Represented by the repetition of efficient, low-cost units closely spaced together, the pattern of land use would very likely be a dense, monotonous cover of small scale buildings. Interesting innovations in mass housing, like the visual community and designs inspired by tribal living, might also be introduced to make these utilitarian residential environments more vibrant and communal.

Dispersed Housing

Children's belt of activities: a new focus and scale of movement in residential communities

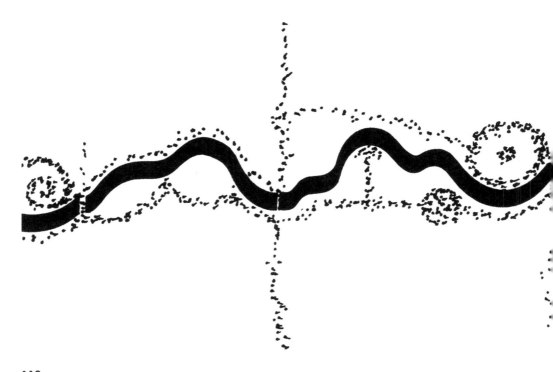

One design idea that is associated with these residential patterns is a children's belt. Its scale is that of a small stream running through a residential neighborhood. Nursery and elementary schools, clinics and centers of pediatric research would be integrated with the housing. In this way a community makes the most use of its educational, health, and general human resources, and offers a new kind of training for its young.

A new, more inclusive concept for residential living is shown between the commercial and government-cultural growth lines. Intended to serve teachers, artists, research and professional persons who do not need to commute daily to a place of work, these residential environments can be much less conventional than other types of housing in the linear society. More attention might be given, for example, to integrating work and living functions and to the interaction of people in the design of private and communal spaces.

This housing design shows a multifamily community which might be composed of ten to twenty units. It provides privacy for the individual families, but stresses the facilities that they share, such as libraries, workshops, day nurseries, laboratories, places for contemplation and for relaxation. The architecture would express the experimental nature of the environment, and would become in some instances pure sculpture.

Often introverted and intensely preoccupied with their own work, artists and intellectuals as a group might be apt to resist conventional concepts of communal living; but on the scale of an intimate social and family life, fellowship seems possible. Sharing facilities and daily life experiences in these multifamily com-

munities would tend to increase communication between persons working together in associated areas
of research and as a result diminish divisive tensions
in the arts and sciences. If multifamily living became
a general practice in a society, projects involving
people in larger numbers and with dissimilar interests
and occupations might be undertaken. Experimentation
of this kind could make the significance of these communal environments extend far beyond national
borders.

As a design idea, the segment represents a contrast of
cross-sectional movement which, for important social
and cultural purposes, can break the dominant longitudinal direction of the growth lines. Originating on
the government-cultural belt, a university or experimental research center could be such a generating
force and gradually grow intense enough to domi-

The Segment

nate an entire cross section. Transitional environments, then, might be needed to prevent the diffusion of these social and cultural energies from subverting the inherent activities of each growth line.

This cross-sectional direction and penetration of influence is expressed visually by the transversal axis that connects associated functions across the segment and could become an exciting experience of counter-movement in a linear society.

An extremely relevant and philosophical segmental activity is designated here as a sparking action. At appointed intervals along the growth lines special communication centers would be established. The computer speeds of these informational and problem-solving processes, relative to ordinary media operations, can be visualized as a superimposed, lightning-type movement taking precedence over them and assumed to travel sporadically and in random patterns throughout the society.

Besides such communication functions, these centers also could perform therapeutic services. Sociologists,

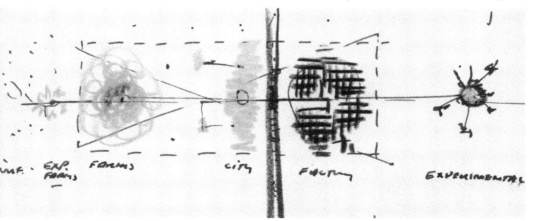

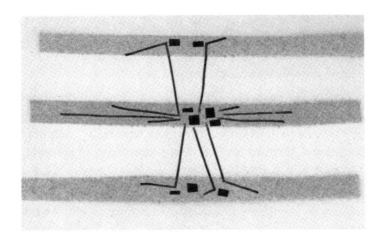

psychologists, and other professionals could use their research facilities to broaden their experiments. Free to bypass all standard procedures and controls, pilot projects could be much less structured than those carried on in conventional research environments. The absence of conforming pressures, of technological and intellectual barriers could result in sudden changes of direction and momentum in scientific and intuitive work without endangering the stability of a society's evolutionary processes.

Architecturally this sparking action can be expressed symbolically. The contact points across the growth lines can be visualized as an instigation of transverse movement with sporadic longitudinal spurs. The segmental cut need not be very wide to be recognizable immediately by members of a society because of the changes of scale and character in the buildings and circulation patterns. A filtering movement would be an appropriate imagery for circulation through the segment because of restricted public access to many of the operations. Strong, machine forms in the landscape would identify the segmental activities, and their super-position in environments would signify the freedom of the society's cerebral processes.

Park Belt

A green belt representing a linear society's free space, the growth line of undeveloped land is reserved for its present needs for recreation and leisure activities and for their future expansion. The visual character of these environments is imagined to vary according to the recreational needs of neighboring growth lines. In this prototype of a linear society, the park belt is shown between the heavy industry and commercial belts as a neutral environmental zone between their intense, often machine-dominated activities. Adjacent to industrial developments, therefore, physical and psychological leisure activities might cater to people wanting repose from the tensions and unbalances of factory environments. On the other hand, near residential con-

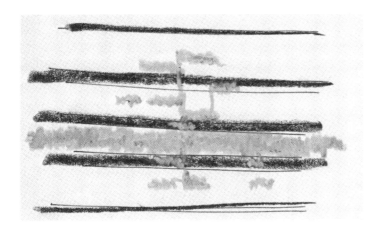

centrations, children's camps and similar recreational environments would be likely to develop in relation to the development of housing. Accordingly the park belt is indicated here as a ribbon of changing activities whose function is to connect the natural landscape with man-made environments.

Routes of cross circulation connecting the park belt with other growth lines could become spurs that penetrate the society with its therapeutic and recreational experiences. Designed to stimulate and refresh, to be areas for rest and the enjoyment of nature, some environments on the park belt might be designed purely as aesthetic and psychological experiences. In these areas sculpture, color, water, and landscape forms, besides providing pleasure also might function symbolically to put people at ease and help to release them from excessive pressures and anxieties. The park belt therefore represents a marked environmental change from other growth lines of a linear society.

**Farm-Industry
Belt**

Representing the boundary of the active, densely populated belts in a linear society, the growth line for farm industry is inherently a transitional environment relating farming and forestry operations with associated activities on the more intensely developed growth lines. Agricultural equipment manufactured in industrial centers of the heavy industry growth line could be assembled and distributed by agencies located on the farm-industry belt. Similarly, farm produce would be processed at marketing centers along the farm-industry belt, presumably at points of interchange with transversal transportation arteries.

The design of circulation, both longitudinal and transversal, is certainly a primary concern. Air transport could be coordinated with highway layouts in order that terminal points work efficiently with local systems of distribution. This kind of interdependency would be critical where perishable foods are processed. Related to the type of farming operations, dairies and silos might be located at important interchanges. These storage facilities, occurring at regular intervals, also would create an obvious visual rhythm giving identification to the farm-industry belt.

Although the linear development of services and manufacturing processes would be determined by the crops grown in a given region and by the subdivision of land, whether owned individually or collectively, agricultural organizations like cooperatives, agricultural institutes, and university extensions are assumed to be typical generators of its environments.

The discharging of a society's intense development into farm and forest regions can be interpreted as the exhaustion of its collective energies. Active use of its land and resources along the principal growth lines

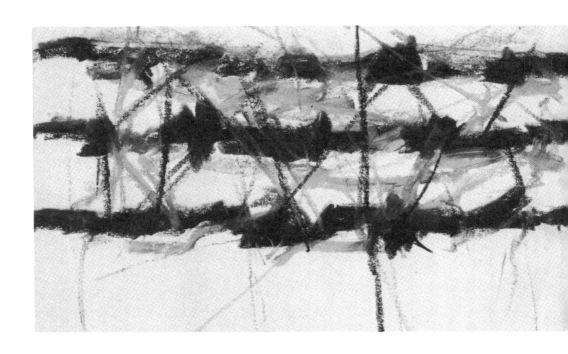

makes it possible as a planning concept to conserve the maximum portion of a nation's territory and allow it to remain in its natural state. The farm-industry belt acts, then, for the society as a boundary—the stopping point of its transversal development—the edge of its formal definition.

This comment also relates to the general philosophy of the linear society, which is to contain the majority of a population's needs, services, and social experiences within clear, expressible limits. Growth is designed for. In the longitudinal direction expansion can be accommodated in a variety of ways but, except at designated segments, transversal development would be opposed, first by the strong momentum of the three most active growth lines and finally by the farm-industry belt, which in the prototype plan of a linear society filters activity at the edges of its cross section.

Variation in the Growth Lines

To adjust to a significant change, either of function or in geographical and climatic conditions, the parallel movement of the growth lines probably would be disrupted. The interpenetrations and crossovers at these points of dislocation might as superpositions initiate new environmental rhythms in a linear society.

Also at borders separating a linear society from neighboring states not sympathetic to continuing this system of development in their territory, the growth lines would be forced to terminate. By design this could happen through a gradual decrease in activity

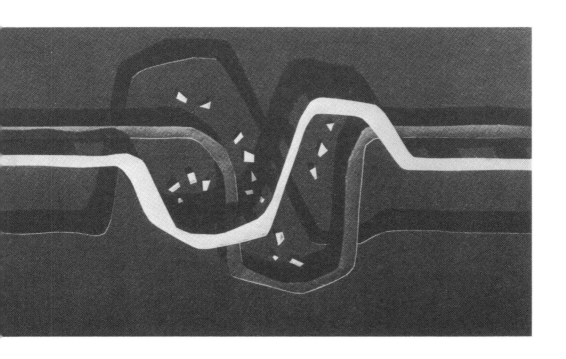

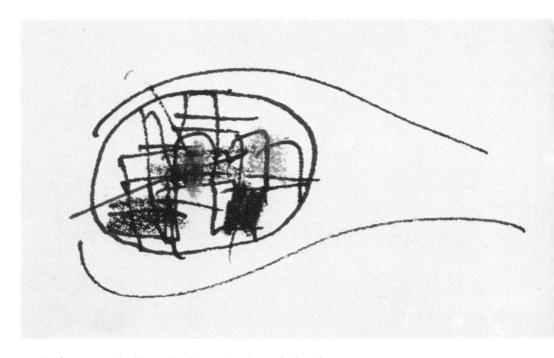

until the growth lines had reached a skeletal state. The sketch shows them ending in a clasping action around a hub, an important terminal and interchange point for the linear society and its neighbor.

With expansion problems becoming more pervasive and threatening during this century than ever before, procedures other than force need to be instituted to contain societies within respected geographical limits. International lines as borders for all societies is one possibility. Considered to be neutral zones, they might be interpreted as a tracery of geographical limits marking off distinct social groupings.

International Growth Lines

Related to the concept of a world of variation, international lines would protect the integrity of societies

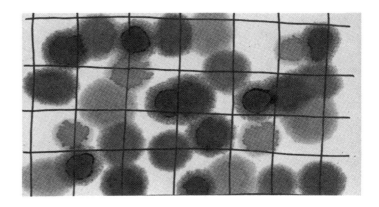

regardless of their size or strength. Associations such as the European Common Market, the Organization of American States, the Pan-Arab and Pan-African organizations that are spreading through their respective continents have already interpreted boundaries among nations in relative terms.

One need not imagine an inflexible pattern imposed on the earth's surface; instead, one can contemplate

design concepts on a planetary scale that incorporate international borders. Barriers, of the order of magnitude of mountain ranges and bodies of water, can be visualized from an international design standpoint as neutral or filtering forms that identify and become transitional environments relating world societies.

A more straightforward intersection, determined by the converging of north, south, east, and west directions of growth lines, might be designed to be a neutral spot, a negative space, in regions of conflict like the Middle East.

By working out a frame of reference which establishes a neutrality between distinct cultures along their physical borders, variation would be protected in their

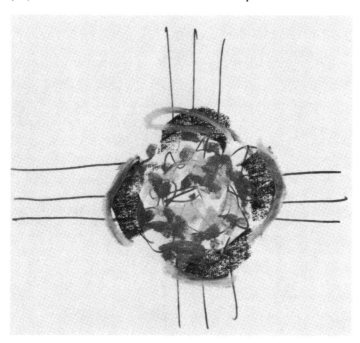

respective cultural developments. Just as without cultural protection the separate states and regions of the United States have lost their original characters, a future union of African or Asian societies could succumb to the domination of a few strong powers.

Assuming that the inner development of societies is not transgressed, an interesting cross-pollination of ideas could happen at border intersections. In this sketch showing a possible intersection of linear societies, a hub of activity results, its architectural expression and circular movement contrasting with the linear character of the intersecting growth lines. Such a nodal point might turn out to be an international city like Geneva and promote the exchange of ideas, products, and diplomatic and cultural functions. In this way international lines would become a means of cultural protection and recognition.

Besides exhibition and supervisory functions, these important contact points might include shared programs of research and technological development. Adjacent small nations, for example, might build atomic energy plants collectively and sponsor joint medical centers, located at such intersection points on international growth lines. The design idea is meant to encourage neighboring societies to combine their most costly and difficult projects with the expectation of raising their domestic standards of living and increasing the prospects of peace among world powers.

CHAPTER 11

A SUMMARY OF IDEAS

It is clear that in the human consciousness there are many images—images from nature of webs, flowers, mountains; images from geometry of circular and linear concepts—which are valuable not only as symbols but potentially as principles of organization.

In present societies many of these emotions and images are expressed only fragmentarily and in contradictory ways. An underlying, consistent, and generic framework, however, could give form and meaning to the potentially self-destructive human world. Consciously developing such a framework for society is both a visual and philosophical task because a society's beliefs and cultural attitudes are implicit in its physical design.

Might physical and social planning, become superimposed rhythms of time and change that are resonant with the actual rhythms of life itself?

Within their frameworks societies, whether old or new, must provide visual and social mechanisms for growth and the evolution of traditions

NOTES AND REFERENCES

PREFACE

A friend of ours, Carl Sapers of Boston, put together the following information concerning the quotation: *"Homo sum: Humani nil a me alienum puto* (Terence, *Heauton Timoroumenos,* 1.77)"* or, in the vulgate, "I am a man and reckon nothing human alien to me."

Lawrence B. Anderson and Jesse R. Fillman are such human beings. We wish to acknowledge their influence on the development of *World of Variation.* "And there always are in the world a few inspired men whose acquaintance is beyond price, and who spring up quite as much in ill-ordered as in well-ordered societies."

—"Laws," XII, 951B, *Dialogues of Plato* (Translated by B. Jowett, Random House, N.Y., 1937)

INTRODUCTION

"Thus we may say that the most lasting contribution to the growth of knowledge that a theory can make are the new problems which it raises, so that we are led back to the view of science and of the growth of knowledge as always starting from, and always ending with, problems—problems of an ever-increasing depth, and an ever-increasing fertility in suggesting new problems. . . . In this way, theories are seen to be free creations of our minds, the results of an almost poetic intuition, of an attempt to understand intuitively the laws of nature."

—Karl R. Popper, *Conjectures and Refutations*

Planning Conditions
of New Societies

Ruth Benedict in *Patterns of Culture* makes many pertinent remarks, among which are the following: "No society has yet attempted a self-conscious direction of the process by which its new normalities are created in the next generation. Dewey has pointed out how possible and yet how drastic such social engineering would be."

The Technological
Approach

Mamadou Dia, economist from Senegal, remarked in *The African Nations and World Solidarity* (Praeger, N.Y., 1961) "Since economy is essentially based on human and social relations, since it is in essence socialistic, in the broadest sense of the term, the role of the accumulation of money—the foundation of capitalism—cannot be the law that will determine the formation of structures in such civilizations. The economist who wishes to do a scientific job, to make an analysis that goes to the heart of the reality, can no longer be content with established schemata, fixed norms, prefabricated models."

Outline of the
Planning Profession

Garden Cities of Tomorrow, by Ebenezer Howard, is a classic work that has influenced twentieth-century architects and planners in Europe and the United States. Both Le Corbusier's "La Ville Radieuse" and Frank Lloyd Wright's "Broadacre City" trace back to Ebenezer Howard's concept and the two communities that he built.

Le Corbusier's plan for Paris in 1934 was an early attempt by the architect to visualize whole cities. His design for Chandigarh in the Punjab, India, has been a successful post-war development of his earlier ideas. Nervi's autostrada del Sole, constructed in the 1960's is a beautiful movement of concrete arches and a highway ribbon piercing a countryside that is mountainous and has changed very little since the Renaissance period. Reminiscent of Roman aqueducts the autostrada gives a scale and continuity to the landscape which does not conflict with but instead connects otherwise discontinuous village settlements.

"Latin America must be realistically considered as a battle-ground upon which we are engaged in a struggle to determine not only the fate of a region, but an entire way of life."

—Juscelino Kubitschek, former president of Brazil (excerpt from a speech made at Harvard University, March 1962)

"My method is to advance by steps, thinking out every step as I go. . . . Naturally we must foresee matters, temper our policies, and allow them to evolve according to both circumstances and means at our disposal."

—Habib Bourguiba (excerpt from a speech made on October 12, 1961, translated and published by the Tunisian Secretariat of State for Information)

"Let us decide not to imitate Europe; let us combine our muscles and our brains in a new direction. Let us try to create the whole man whom Europe has been incapable of bringing to triumphant birth."

—Franz Fanon, *The Wretched of the Earth*

"Perhaps we can consider the revolutionary effort of the despised masses of the colonial, semi-colonial, and dependent countries as the most important event of this century."

—Abel Alexis Latendorf, Argentina (excerpt from an interview by Carlos Strasser in *Las Izquierdas en el Proceso Politico Argentino*, Buenos Aires, Editorial Palestra, 1959)

PART I

A FRAMEWORK FOR IDEAS

Chapter 1
HUMAN VARIABLES

The Problem of Time

"Although we human beings have our own personal life, we are yet in large measure the representatives, the victims and promoters of a collective spirit whose years are counted in centuries."

—C.J. Jung, *Memories, Dreams, Reflections*

This expresses the contrasting scales of time which the individual is affected by and is conscious of at different times and on various levels of awareness. It is noteworthy that the probable duration of a human life in the modern world is eight hundred months, but a cultural phase can last as many years. "As Lenin once remarked, 'There are centuries that pass as if they were days—and there are days that pass as if they were centuries.' The latter calendar clearly rules in these times."

—Michael Harrington, *The Accidental Century*

A.N. Whitehead in his philosophical writings, particularly *The Adventure of Ideas*, was preoccupied with time, how the realm of the timeless, what he termed "eternal objects," ingressed into history. Like Marx, Whitehead was influenced by Hegel in approaching the problem of how ideas become expressed in the flux of events, the dynamic movement of thesis-antithesis-synthesis.

"Time present and time past
Are both perhaps present in time future,
And time future contained in time past.
....
What might have been and what has been
Point to one end, which is always present."

T.S. Eliot, "Burnt Norton," *Four Quartets*

"I realized from the outset that our success depended on our complete understanding of the nature of the circumstances in which we live in the present phase of our country's history."

—Gamal Abdel Nasser (excerpt from *The Philosophy of Revolution*, Cairo Information Department, 1954)

Process of Change

Brasilia, the capital city of Brazil, was designed principally by Oscar Niemeyer and was constructed rapidly under the Kubitschek Administration. The purpose of removing the capital from Rio de Janeiro was to turn the direction of development

130

of the country inland. A site was chosen in the middle of the plateau, typical of the inland portion of Brazil, and personnel and building materials were transported at first by air. A bold idea, it took tenacity on the part of the designers and administrators to execute. Whether Brasilia achieves its purpose is still unproven. At the very least, however, it arouses economic and cultural interest in Brazil's unexplored potentialities.

The Permanent and Temporary in a Culture

"With culture, something completely new came into the world: the potential immortality of thought, of truth, of knowledge. An entire people, an entire race, can now perish, and yet their culture can survive in libraries—so that another people, even another planet, can find it and make use of it. This is the real immortality of the spirit. . . . But on the other hand, culture can die even though men survive, and that's what threatens us today, because the growth, the expansion, of this immense body of cumulative knowledge requires brains, books, and traditions. Culture is not something that soars over men's heads. It is man himself."

—Interview with Konrad Lorenz, *New York Times Magazine,* July 5, 1970

Traditions

T.S. Eliot, in a series of lectures given at the University of Virginia, in 1933, made the following remarks about traditions: "What I mean by tradition involves all those habitual actions, habits and customs, from the most significant religious rite to our conventional way of greeting a stranger, which represent the blood kinship of 'the same people living in the same place.' "

. . . "I hold—in summing up—that a tradition is rather a way of feeling and acting which characterizes a group throughout generations; and that it must largely be, or that many of the elements in it must be, unconscious."

—T.S. Eliot, *After Strange Gods*

Chapter 2
HUMAN DIMENSIONS

"Certainly the properties to which the savage mind has access are not the same as those which have commanded the attention of scientists. The physical world is approached from opposite ends in the two cases: one is supremely concrete, the other supremely abstract. . . . We have had to wait until the middle of this century for the crossing of long separated paths: that which arrives at the physical world by the detour of communication, and that which as we have recently come to know, arrives at the world of communication by the detour of the physical. The entire process of human knowledge thus assumes the character of a closed system."
—Claude Lévi-Strauss, *The Savage Mind*

Social Uses of Geometry

Suzanne Langer, Ernst Cassirer, Erwin Panofsky, among other philosophers, have been concerned with man's symbolic forms, especially those expressed in the arts, religions, and myths. C.J. Jung in his book, *Symbol and Psyche*, was interested in the unconscious aspects of myth and symbolism and how they are expressed in civilizations. Many of the sketches in *World of Variation* make use of symbolic communication.

Grid Form

Paestum and Pompeii, Greek and Roman settlements respectively on the Italian peninsula, were laid out upon grid lines. The rectilinear architecture of the temples and forums emphasized the grid pattern of streets and open spaces. Today the ruins give the visitor the visual impression of a three-dimensional checkerboard. Even so, the size of a Greek or Roman city (often 10,000 inhabitants) was small relative to that of cities of the modern epoch, so that the grid form did not become oppressive, inflexible, or monotonous. Besides, coliseums and amphitheatres, and other significant urban forms offset the scale and grid character of the ordinary working and residential environments. In comparison a modern city, such as New York, is so large that even monuments and civic centers, parks and open spaces (except those like Central Park which then are too large to be

132

experienced as a form) cannot compete with the uniform and expanding grid of streets and buildings. The vertical repetition of grid lines in the architectural treatment of skyscrapers reiterates the anonymity of the total grid environment.

Supra-Rational Form

"Our concepts of space and time have only approximate validity, and there is therefore a wide field for minor and major deviations. In view of all this I lend an attentive ear to the strange myths of the psyche, and take a careful look at the varied events that come my way, regardless of whether or not they fit in with my theoretical postulates. . . . These experiments prove that the psyche at times functions outside of the spatio-temporal law of causality. This indicates that our conceptions of space and time, and therefore of causality also, are incomplete."

   —C.J. Jung, *Memories, Dreams, Reflections*

Chapter 3
HUMAN ADAPTATIONS

"There does seem to be unlimited knowledge present in nature, it is true, but it can be comprehended by consciousness only when the time is ripe for it. The process, presumably, is like what happens in the individual psyche: a man may go about for many years with an inkling of something, but grasps it clearly only at a particular moment."

   —C.J. Jung, *Memories, Dreams, Reflections*

Images from Nature

W.R. Lethaby has explored the natural world as sources of architectural expressions, especially those related to very sacred functions, like temples and tombs. Magic and religious rituals were traced by Lethaby to experiences of nature, which in turn became the sources of inspiration for men's art forms including architecture. A similar kind of visual correspondence between qualities in nature and those within man has been explored by Ingmar Bergman in his films.

Land Forms

Gyorgy Kepes in *The New Landscape* shows interesting photographs of land forms from the air. As an artist he has been inspired by the new possibilities of perceiving nature in the twentieth century.

Chapter 4
HUMAN PROTECTIONS

"These concepts are based on the assumption that psychological and social phenomena can be represented in psychological and social 'space.' So we speak of the 'life-space' of an individual or the 'social space' of a group. The life space of an individual and the social space of a group may be regarded as systems which are stratified into regions. These regions vary qualitatively and are separated from one another by boundaries more or less previous. Everything that has an effect on a person is part of his life spaces."
—John Cohen, "Analysis of Psychological Fields" (*Science News*)

The Need for
Psychological
Protections

"We must keep a sense of proportion about it. Some people seem to think tribalism is an unmitigated evil, but it is not. Every ethnic group has its own cultural features and may, therefore, have something of value to contribute to the way of life of the country or region of which it forms a part. The American of British stock, the Irish-American, the American Jew, the American Negro, and all the other tribes that compose the American nation, have contributed in different ways to make the American culture what it is today.... The same has happened, and is happening in Africa. There you will find that each tribe is well known for one distinctive quality. It may be industriousness, or brains, or a flair for commerce, or political sagacity, or a gift for diplomacy, or a sense of humor, or even a love of gaiety. Whatever it is, it serves to enrich the national cultural pattern."
—S.O. Adebo, excerpt from "*An African Chief explains Tribalism*" (The New York Times Magazine, March 1, 1964)

PART II

ARCHITECTURE ON A SOCIAL SCALE

Chapter 5
SOCIAL CONCERNS

"Unearned suffering is redemptive"
—Martin Luther King, *Pilgrimage to Nonviolence*
"I now see that sorrow, being the supreme emotion of which
man is capable, is at once the type and test of all great art.
What the artist is always looking for is the mode of existence
in which soul and body are one and indivisible: in which the
outward is expressive of the inward: in which form reveals."
—Oscar Wilde, *De Profundis*

The Need for Fantasy

In reference to the lack of well being in environments in the
United States and to the corresponding need for compensa-
tions, Karl Meninger in *Man Against Himself*, asserts that self-
destructiveness "comes about as a result of (apparently) in-
superable difficulties in adjusting one's self to the complexities
of the environment. . . . "It is therefore appropriate that we
give some consideration to another point of view, namely, that
some change in the organization or structure of a society might
accomplish something of benefit to the individuals who compose
it, in the direction of lessening the necessity for self-destruction."

Forms and Spaces
Understood through
the Unconscious

"The denuding of conscious life and its reduction to a single
level created the new world of the unconscious in the seventeenth century. The stage has been cleared of the archetypes
or postures of individual mind, and is ready for the archetypes of the collective unconscious."
—Marshall McLuhan, *The Gutenberg Galaxy*

Based on his own prison experience Oscar Wilde made these observations in *De Profundis:*

On Prisons: "It is not the prisoners who need reformation. It is the prisons."

The Life of the Prisoner: "For us there is only one season, the season of sorrow. The very sun and moon seem taken from us. . . . It is always twilight in one's cell, as it is always twilight in one's heart. And in the sphere of thought, no less than in the sphere of time, motion is no more."

The Viewpoint of the Poor to the Prisoner: "The poor are wiser, more charitable, more kind, more sensitive than we are. In their eyes prison is a tragedy in a man's life, a misfortune, a casualty, something that calls for sympathy in others. They speak of one who is in prison as of one who is 'in trouble,' simply. It is the phrase they always use, and the expression has the perfect wisdom of love in it."

The Return of the Prisoner to Society: "Many men on their release carry their prison about with them into the air, and hide it as a secret disgrace in their hearts, and at length, like poor poisoned things, creep into some hole and die. It is wretched that they should have to do so, and it is wrong, terribly wrong, of society that it should force them to do so. . . . Society takes upon itself the right to inflict appalling punishment on the individual, but it also has the supreme vice of shallowness, and fails to realize what it has done. When the man's punishment is over, it leaves him to himself; that is to say, it abandons him at the very moment when its highest duty towards him begins. It is really ashamed of its own actions, and shuns those whom it has punished, as people shun a creditor whose debt they cannot pay, or one on whom they have inflicted an unreparable, an irredeemable wrong."

The contemporary relevancy of these remarks shows that neither attitudes toward nor the conditions of prison life have changed. "Malcolm X had a special meaning for black convicts. A former prisoner himself, he had risen from the lowest depths to great heights. For this reason he was a symbol of hope, a model for thousands of black convicts who found themselves trapped in the vicious PPP cycle: prison-parole-prison. One thing that the judges, policemen, and administrators of prisons seem never to have understood, and for which they certainly do not make any allowances, is that Negro convicts, basically, rather than see themselves as criminals and perpetrators of misdeeds, look upon themselves as prisoners of war, the victims of a vicious, dog-eat-dog social system that is so heinous as to cancel out their own malefactions: in the jungle there is no right or wrong."

—Eldridge Cleaver, *Soul on Ice*

A Society's Treatment of Non-Conformity

Freud, in his book, *Civilization and its Discontents* brings out the growing human conflict between the desire for civilization and the aversion toward the repressive procedures that are its necessary counterparts. As Stephen Lestrange said in an article, "Group Psychotherapy" in *Science News*, Volume 8, 1948, "Freud recognized that neurosis was largely, if not entirely, a price that was paid for civilization and the many advantages gained from a complex social organization."

The need to protect the individuality of groups and cultures from domination by a social majority is emphasized by Ruth Benedict, in her book, *Patterns of Culture:* "The vast proportion of all individuals who are born into any society always and whatever the idiosyncrasies of its institutions, assume as we have seen the behavior dictated by the society.... Most people are shaped to the form of their culture because of the enormous malleability of their original endowment. They are plastic to the moulding force of the society into which they are born.... They do not all, however, find it equally congenial, and those are favoured and fortunate whose potentialities most nearly coincide with the type of behavior selected by their society.... Most ethnologists have had similar experiences in recognizing that the persons who are put outside the pale of society with contempt are not those who would be placed there by another culture."

A Study of Family Life

Ravello, a hilltop village 1200 feet above Amalfi in Southern Italy, represents an agricultural community whose basic life rhythms have continued undisturbed through centuries. Each family member works at a task like performing a part in a play. The role has been ritualistically rehearsed. One sees an old woman, obviously the grandmother and matriarch, on an upstairs balcony of the old stone farmhouse airing blankets and at the same time, supervising the activities and conversations of her progeny below. A younger woman hangs out wash on a line and talks with a contemporary, either husband or brother, who is pruning vines. The oldest man, the grandfather and visibly the head of the family, directs a group of eight or ten younger men—sons, grandsons, and sons-in-law,—who are repairing stakes and lattices of the family vineyard. Girls in their teens and early twenties—the wives, sisters, and daughters, of the men working—weed vegetables in plots further away from the house. Then several levels below the farmhouse on less tillable land, children play as they keep watch on the family's herd of animals.

An observer looking across the Valley of the Dragone at such a family at work on their land cannot help but become aware of the structure of family life that has been the source, the basic imagery of Western civilization.

Chapter 6
COMMUNAL INNOVATIONS

The Problem of Connection
"This is our basic conclusion: our nation is moving toward two societies, one black, one white—separate and unequal."
  —Report of the National Advisory Commission on Civil Disorders

Group Conflicts
"We have cited deep hostility between police and ghetto communities as a primary cause of the disorders surveyed by the Commission. . . . The true extent of excessive and unjustified use of force is difficult to determine. . . . There are at least three serious problems involved in the use of deadly weapons in a civil disorder. The first is the risk of killing or wounding in-

nocent persons—bystanders or passersby who may in fact be hundreds of feet away when a shot is fired. . . . The second is the justification for the use of deadly force against crimes like looting. . . . The third problem is that the use of excessive force—the inappropriate display of weapons—may be inflammatory and lead to even worse disorders."

—*Report of the National Advisory Commission on Civil Disorders*

"It is incorrect to classify the revolt of the Negro as simply a racial conflict of black against white, or as a purely American problem. Rather, we are today seeing a global rebellion of the oppressed against the oppressor, the exploited against the exploiter."

—Malcolm X (excerpt from his speech "The Black Revolution and its effect upon Negroes of the Western Hemisphere," given at Columbia University on February 18, 1965)

Chapter 7
COMMUNAL FORMS

Concept of Subsidiary Societies

Concerning experimental areas in a society, there can be many more techniques and kinds of experimentation than have been previously undertaken. "There is no particular method of enquiry appropriate for the sociologist. He will choose the method of approach and the specialized hypotheses with which he is concerned. . . . When the sociologist studies an individual or group of people he often needs to watch their behavior in a number of different situations."

—Anthony H. Richmond, "Social Scientists in Action" (*Science News*, Vol. 25, 1953)

Growth Rings: an evolutionary community

"The more mechanical people to whom life is a shrewd speculation depending on a careful calculation of ways and means, always know where they are going, and go there. . . . But with the dynamic forces of life, and those in whom those dynamic forces become incarnate, it is different. People whose desire is solely for self-realization never know where they are going. They can't know. In one sense of the word it is of course necessary, as the Greek oracle said, to know oneself: That is the first achievement of knowledge. But to recognize that the soul of a man is unknowable, that is the ultimate achievement of wisdom. The final mystery is oneself. When one has weighed the sun in the balance, and measured the steps of the moon, and mapped out the seven heavens star by star, there still remains oneself. Who can calculate the orbit of his own soul?"

— Oscar Wilde, *De Profundis*

PART III

ARCHITECTURE BEYOND CITIES

Chapter 8
MASS AND INDIVIDUAL SCALE MOVEMENT IN SOCIETY

"The people, and the people alone, are the motive force in the making of world history."

Mao Tse-Tung, *Quotations from Chairman Mao Tse-Tung*

**Mass Scale
Movements**

"Every healthy democracy should rest on the liberation of the people."

—Gamal Abdel Nasser (excerpt from speech delivered at the opening of the High Dam Project, November 26, 1959. English translation from *Nasser's Speeches and Press Interviews*, 1959)

"As society has changed, so has the crowd changed with it and, in changing, has left its legacy to succeeding generations. . . . Of course, there is all the difference in the world between these two approaches—that of Michelet, which sees the crowd as 'the people,' and that of Burke and Taine, which presents the crowd as 'rabble'—yet, in relation to my present argument, they have an important element in common. It is that they both are stereotypes and both present the crowd as a disembodied abstraction and not as an aggregate of men and women of flesh and blood."

—George Rude, *The Crowd in History*

140

"All of us are the party of Allah, the party of right and justice. We are the party of struggle. . . . We cannot be disunited by anyone. The people as a whole, and I, being with the people, are making a tremendous revolution undermining imperialism and threatening its structure. . . . We are the party of right and justice. You are the party of right and justice. You are the party of the revolution. You work in the way of Allah and the way of the people to secure the gains of the immortal Iraqui Revolution."

—Abdul Karim Kassem, Iraq (excerpt from speech made May 1, 1959, reprinted from *Principles of 14th July Revolution*, Baghdad, 1959)

"The 'masses' are perhaps the most dramatic illustration of what can happen when a world-historical revolution is accidental. . . . Without rational human direction the accidental revolution is not moving toward a rebirth of poetry but toward an inhuman collectivism."

—Michael Harrington, *The Accidental Century*

Spaces designed for Mass-Scale Movement

"Direction is essential for the continuing existence of the crowd. Its constant fear of disintegration means that it will accept any goal. A crowd exists as long as it has an unattained goal."

—Elias Canetti, *Crowds and Power*

The Idea of a Total Living Space

"In the seventeenth century, and also in the fifteenth and sixteenth centuries, a big house was always crowded with more people in it than little houses. This is an important point, which emerges from all the investigations into density of population made by demographic historians. . . . The big house fulfilled a public function. In that society (17th century) without a café or a 'public house,' it was the only place where friends, clients, relatives, and protégés could meet and talk. . . . There were no professional premises, either for the judge or the merchant or the banker or the business man. . . . People lived in general-

141

purpose rooms. They ate in them, but not at special tables: the 'dining table' did not exist. . . . In the same rooms where they ate, people slept, danced, worked, and received visitors. . . . Now these rooms were no more equipped for domestic work than they were for professional purposes. They communicated with each other, and the richer houses had galleries on the floor where the family lived. On the other floors the rooms were smaller, but just as dependent on one another. None had a special function, except the kitchen, and even the cooking was often done in the hearth in the biggest room."

—Philippe Aries, *Centuries of Childhood*

"Man in Africa does not seek seclusion within isolated rooms but, on the contrary, he strives for permanent contact with nature and with the community. Building in Africa therefore means the creation of a focal point open to all for the development of community living. This fact must also be continually in mind when one considers the creation of a modern African architecture."

—Udo Kultermann, *New Architecture in Africa*

"So it is at the point in history at which the Western work ethic is finally in sight of subverting almost every remnant of tribalism, feudalism, and aristocracy on the globe, it ceases to be a practical guide for the culture that gave it birth."

Michael Harrington, *The Accidental Century*

Chapter 9
THE CONSTRUCTION OF NEW SOCIETIES

New Design Scales
and Purposes

"What other countries have taken three hundred years to achieve, a once-dependent territory must try to accomplish in a generation if it is to survive."

—Kwame Nkrumah, *Ghana: The Autobiography of Kwame Nkrumah*

"Now all African countries have finally taken the road toward independence. This situation creates a certain number of problems to be resolved by African political leaders. We are the so-called underdeveloped countries. We are aware of our economic backwardness. We are aware of our cultural backwardness. . . . For us the essential thing is to mobilize all the forces of the country to advance, and we do not think that liberty is threatened in Africa."

—Madeira Keita, Mali, "Le Parti Unique en Afrique" (*Presence Africaine*, No. 30, 1960)

"It is often overlooked that the Anglo-Saxon tradition of a two-party system is a reflection of the society in which it evolved. Within that society there was a struggle between the 'haves' and 'have-nots' each of whom organized themselves into political parties. . . . With rare exceptions, the idea of class is something entirely alien to Africa."

—Julius Nyere, Tanzania, *Spearhead* (Dar-es-Salaam, 1961)

"If the problem of the individual is a central concern in other continents—in the countries that are free and independent—the first and only true problem for the colonial peoples is that of the attainment of independence. It is consequently a collective problem, a political reality engendered by nationalist sentiments."

—Sekou Touré, Guinea, *La Lutte du Parti Democratique de Guinee pour L'Emancipation Africani* (Imprimerie Nationale, 1959)

Chapter 10
DESIGN OF A LINEAR SOCIETY

Concept of Growth Lines

"The investment of public income cannot be carried out, in our opinion, without a system of planning, without a coherent plan. . . . Democratic planning means the orientation of public investments in accord with a strict system of priorities and the creation of an atmosphere favorable to private activities that are productive of wealth. . . a system for the rational application of fiscal resources and the orientation of private capital in directions useful for the whole community."

—Romulo Betancourt, Venezuela, *Posición y Doctrina* (Edition Cordillera, Caracas, 1959)

The Evolution of
Growth Lines

"Now, if African unity is ever to be more than a beautiful idea, one of the first necessities is a transport system that will open up the continent. Only then will it become possible for the people of the forty-odd countries to know each other, to pursue their common economic, political, and cultural objectives, and defend their common military interests. It would be primarily a highway system, in view of the much greater cost of building and running a comparable railway network and because of the many obstacles to the development of water transport."

—George H.T. Kimble, A "U.S. of Africa"?—Not Very Likely (New York Times Magazine, March 29, 1964)

"Although it was hardly the intention of the dictator, these highways, with all their imperfections, contributed to bringing Venezuelans together and establishing links among them. They basically undermined one of the negative factors in our history, the interregional rivalries and struggles among the states, which were based on the lack of contact and mutual acquaintances among the various regions of a country like ours, with a population that numbers less than four million inhabitants and is dispersed throughout an immense geographical area of 625,000 square miles."

—Romulo Betancourt, Posición y Doctrina

Planning Assumptions
of the Linear Society

"The single or dominant party system is said to be more democratic than a system of two or more parties, since the Western parties usually represent narrow class, religious, or ethnic interests rather than the nation as a whole. . . . The socialism of developing nations is said to be directed at the establishment of a society based on justice rather than profit, rational planning rather than the blind operation of the market, and forced economic growth and industrialization as opposed to the orientation of the economy to the production of raw materials for the profit of foreign enterprises. These goals are accepted by nearly all the leaders of Asia, Africa, Latin America, and the

Middle East, although their implementation is not commonly agreed upon or even understood."
—Paul E. Sigmund, Jr., *The Ideologies of Developing Nations*

"I believe that no underdeveloped country can afford to be anything but socialist. I think, therefore, that we in Africa are bound to organize ourselves on a socialist pattern. But let us at least provide another corrective to socialism, and prevent the wealth we are beginning to build in our own countries from being used for the purpose of acquiring national power or prestige. Let us make sure that it is used solely for raising the standards of our people."
—Julius Nyere, Tanzania, *Spearhead*

"It can hardly be challenged that, in the context of the modern world, no country can be politically and economically independent, even within the framework of international interdependence, unless it is highly industrialized and has developed its power resources to the utmost. Nor can it achieve or maintain high standards of living and liquidate poverty without the aid of modern technology in almost every sphere of life."
—Jawaharlal Nehru, *The Discovery of India*

Government-
Cultural Belt
"Closely studying the social history of rural communes and medieval towns, Kropotkin concluded that men did not have to be ruled."
—Paul Goodman, *Preface to Memoirs of a Revolutionist*

Commercial Belt
"The great importance attached to the role of the public sector, however, cannot do away with the existence of the private sector. The private sector has its effective role in the development plan. . . . By encouraging free competition within the framework of the general economic planning, the private sector is also an invigorating element to the public sector."
—Gamal Abdel Nasser, Egypt (excerpt from his speech on the draft charter, May 21, 1962, U.A.R. Information Department, Cairo)

Children's Belt

"We get an interesting sidelight on this from Dr. Eisenstadt, under whose guidance a considerable amount of social research is carried on in Israel. Among the traditional Oriental families, in which occupation is tied to family life, there is a complete absence of 'youth culture.' In the co-operative settlements (Moshav and Moshava), where the family is still the unit of production, but where there is a certain amount of non-agricultural specialization, there is a certain amount of independent youth activity. In the cities, where there is still more discontinuity between family life and occupation, there is still more, while youth organizations reach their peak in the Kibbutzim, or communal farms, where family life is at a minimum and children live a great part of their lives away from their parents. The 'pioneer' atmosphere in Israel is such that most youth groups, formal and informal, are idealistic, save among the poorer classes, when they tend to be deviant."

—W.J.H. Sprott, *Human Groups*

Concept of the Segment

"The new electronic interdependence recreates the world in the image of a global village."

—Marshall McLuhan, *The Gutenberg Galaxy*

Park Belt

"Abundance could be the prelude to bread and circuses. A degrading leisure would be society's substitute for a degrading work. Some of these possibilities have already been outlined. On the other hand, there could be a new kind of leisure and a new kind of work, or more precisely, a range of activities that would partake of the nature of both leisure and work."

—Michael Harrington, *The Accidental Century*

Farm-Industry Belt

"We favor a system of agrarian reform under which the land will be collectivized and granted to agricultural cooperatives which will be responsible for its management and exploitation."

—Ahmed Ben Bella, Algeria (*excerpt from an interview of Ben Bella with Maria Macchochi*, correspondent for L'Unita, August 13, 1962)

146

"The experts who represent the Monrovia African States met at Dakar and recommended, among other things, the promotion of trade among African countries—through a regional customs union, the introduction of a common external tariff, harmonized policies of economic development, the establishment of a network of roads and other communications linking contiguous African countries, the exchange of economic information, and the founding of an African development bank."

—Nnamdi Azikiwe, Nigeria (excerpt from a speech delivered to Lagos Conference, January 25, 1962)

International Lines

"Whenever we try to talk in terms of larger units on the African continent, we are told that it can't be done; we are told that the units we would so create would be 'artificial.' As if they could be any more artificial than the 'national' units on which we are now building! ... If an African state is armed realistically, it can only be armed against another African state. I think we should be very careful about this. We must not find ourselves committing the same mistakes committed by the nation-states of other continents.... All that we need within our national boundaries are sufficient police forces for the purpose of maintaining law and order within those boundaries."

—Julius Nyere, Tanzania (Excerpt from a speech delivered to the Second Pan-African Seminar, 1961)

Chapter 11

Summary of Ideas

The critical nature of forming cultures is expressed well in the following remark: "The most beautiful as well as the most ugly inclinations of man are not part of a fixed and biologically given human nature, but result from the social process which creates man. In other words, society has not only a supressing function—although it has that too—but it has also a creative function. Man's nature, his passions and anxieties, are a cultural product; as a matter of fact, man himself is the most important creation and achievement of the continuous human effort, the record of which we call history."

—Jan Ehrenwald, M.D., *From Medicine Man to Freud*

BIBLIOGRAPHY

Agee, James, *Let Us Now Praise Famous Men*, Houghton Mifflin Co., Boston, 1941

Ardrey, Robert, *The Territorial Imperative*, Atheneum,
New York, 1966

Atkinson, Richard, *Stonehenge*, Macmillan, New York,
1956

Baudelaire, Charles, *The Mirror of Art*, Doubleday
Anchor Books, New York, 1956

Benedict, Ruth, *Patterns of Culture*, Houghton Mifflin
Co., Boston, 1934

Berne, Eric, *The Structure and Dynamics of Organizations and Groups*, Grove Press, New York, 1966

Bonham-Carter, Victor, *The English Village*, Penguin
Books, New York, 1952

Bowlby, John, *New Biology*, Penguin Books, New York,
1953

Brill, A.A., M.D., *Psychoanalytic Psychiatry*, A.A. Knopf,
New York, 1946

Burnett Tylor, Sir Edward, *The Origins of Culture*,
Harper & Row, New York, 1958

Butcher, Margaret J., *The Negro in American Culture*,
A.A. Knopf, New York, 1956

Butler, J.A.V., *Science News*, Penguin Books, New
York, 1951

Bychowski, Gustave, *Specialized Techniques in Psycho-
Therapy*, Grune & Stratton, New York, 1952

Cannetti, Elias, *Crowds and Power*, Viking Press, New York, 1962

Cassirer, Ernst, *An Essay on Man*, Oxford University Press, New York, 1944

Cassirer, Ernst, *The Philosophy of Symbolic Forms*, Yale University Press, New Haven, Conn., 1953

Childs, Marquis W., *Sweden the Middle Way*, Yale University Press, New Haven, Conn., 1936

Chomsky, Noam, *Language and Mind*, Harcourt, Brace & World, New York, 1968

Cleaver, Eldridge, *Soul on Ice*, Dell Publishing Co., New York, 1968

Cohen, Dr. John, *Science News*, Penguin Books, New York, 1949

Coulton, G.G., *Medieval Faith and Symbolism*, Harper & Row, New York, 1958

Daedalus, *The Future Metropolis*, American Academy of Arts and Sciences, Cambridge, Mass., Winter 1961

Dolci, Danilo, *The Outlaws of Partnico*, MacGibbon & Kee, London, 1960

Edwards, I.E.S., *The Pyramids of Egypt*, Penguin Books, New York, 1952

Ehrenwald, Jan, M.D., *From Medicine Man to Freud*, Dell Publishing Co., New York, 1956

Ehrenzweig, Anton, *The Psycho-Analysis of Artistic Vision and Hearing*, Routledge & Paul, London, 1953

Eliot, T.S., *After Strange Gods*, Harcourt, Brace & World, New York, 1934

Eliot, T.S., *Four Quartets*, Harcourt, Brace & World, New York, 1943

Elkin, A.P., *The Australian Aborigines*, Natural History Library Edition, New York, 1964

Evans, Walker, *American Photographs*, Museum of Modern Art, New York, 1938

Fannon, Frantz, *The Wretched of the Earth*, Grove Press Inc., New York, 1968

Fraser, Douglas, *Village Planning in Primitive Societies*, George Braziller, New York, 1968

Freed, Leonard, *Black in White America*, Grossman Publishers, New York, 1968

Freud, Sigmund, *Civilization and Its Discontents*, Hogarth Press, London, 1930

Fry, Roger, *Vision and Design*, Brentano, New York, 1922

Giedion, Sigfried, *Time, Space and Architecture*, Harvard University Press, Cambridge, Mass., 1941

Goodman, Paul, *Growing Up Absurd*, Random House, New York, 1960

Goodman, Percival and Paul, *Communitas*, Vintage Books, New York, 1960

Gorky, Maxim, *The Lower Depths*, Yale University Press, New Haven, Conn., 1945

Greenough, Horatio, *Form and Function*, University of California Press, Berkeley, 1947

Guevara, Che, *Guerilla Warfare*, Random House, New York, 1961

Handlin, Oscar, *The Uprooted*, Little-Brown, Boston, 1951

Harrington, Michael, *The Accidental Century*, Penguin Books, New York, 1966

Hilberseimer, L., *The Nature of Cities*, Paul Theobald & Co., Chicago, 1955

Hilberseimer, L., *The Regional Pattern*, Paul Theobald & Co., Chicago, 1949

Hilgard, Ernest R., *Psychoanalysis As Science*, Stanford University Press, Stanford, Calif., 1952

Hiorns, Frederick, *Town Building in History*, Harrap, London, 1956

Hirsch, Werner Z., *Urban Life and Form*, Henry Holt & Co., New York, 1963

Hoffer, Eric, *The True Believer*, Harper & Bros., New York, 1951

Howard, Ebenezer, *Garden Cities of Tomorrow*, Faber & Faber Ltd., London, 1946

Huxley, Aldous, *Brave New World*, Harper & Bros., New York, 1946

Jammer, Max, *Concepts of Space*, Harvard University Press, Cambridge, Mass., 1957

Jones, Maxwell, *Social Psychiatry, a Study of Therapeutic Communities*, Routledge, Kegan, & Paul, London, 1952

Jung, C.J., *Memories, Dreams, Reflections*, Pantheon Books, New York, 1963

Jung, C.J., *Psyche & Symbol*, Doubleday, New York, 1958

Keats, John, *The Crack in the Picture Window*, Ballantine Books, New York, 1956

Kepes, Gyorgy, *The New Landscape*, Paul Theobald & Co., Chicago, 1956

King, Martin Luther, *Pilgrimage to Nonviolence*, Bobbs-Merrill, New York, 1965

Klare, Hugh J., *Anatomy of Prison*, Penguin Books, New York, 1960

Kluckholn, Clyde, *Mirror For Man*, Whittlesey House, New York, 1949

Kohler, Wolfgang, *Gestalt Psychology*, Liverright Publishing Co., New York, 1947

Kris, Ernst, *Psychoanalytic Explorations in Art*, International Universities Press, New York, 1952

Kropotkin, Peter, *Memoirs of a Revolutionist*, Grove Press Inc., New York, 1970

Kultermann, Udo, *New Architecture in Africa*, Universe Books, New York, 1963

Langer, Susanne K., *Feeling and Form*, Scribner's, New York, 1953

Langer, Susanne K., *Philosophy in a New Key*, Harvard University Press, Cambridge, Mass., 1942

Larrabee, Eric, *Mass Leisure*, Free Press, Glencoe, Illinois, 1958

Le Corbusier, *Concerning Town Planning*, London Architectural Press, London, 1947

Le Corbusier, *The City of Tomorrow*, London Architectural Press, London, 1948

Le Corbusier, *The Home of Man*, The Architectural Press, London, 1948

Le Corbusier, *Towards a New Architecture*, Payson & Clarke, Ltd., London, 1927

Lenin, V.I., *What Is To Be Done*, International Publishers, New York, 1929

Lestrange, Stephen, *Science News*, Penguin Books, New York, 1948

Lethaby, W.R., *Architecture, Nature & Magic*, Gerald Duckworth & Co. Ltd., London, 1956

Lethaby, W.R., *Form in Civilization*, Oxford University Press, New York, 1957

Lévi-Strauss, Claude, *The Savage Mind*, University of Chicago Press, Chicago, 1966

Lippmann, Walter, *The Public Philosophy*, Little-Brown, Boston, 1955

Lorenz, Konrad, *On Aggression*, Harcourt, Brace & World, Inc., New York, 1966

Lowenfeld, Viktor, *The Nature of Creative Activity*, L. Routledge, London, 1952

Lucretius, *The Nature of the Universe*, Penguin Classics, New York, 1952

Luttwak, Edward, *Coup D'Etat*, Fawcett Premier Books, Greenwich, Conn., 1960

Malcolm X, *Autobiography of Malcolm X*, Grove Press, Inc., New York, 1965

Malinowski, Bronislaw, *Magic, Science, and Religion*, Doubleday, New York, 1948

Mallet, Robert, *Jardins et Paradis*, Librairie Gallimard, Paris, 1959

Mann, Ida, *The Science of Seeing*, Pelican Book, London, 1950

Mannheim, Karl, *Ideology and Utopia*, Harcourt, Brace & Co., New York, 1940

Marcuse, Herbert, *One Dimensional Man*, Beacon Press, Boston, 1968

Marcuse, Herbert, *Reason As Revolution*, Beacon Press, Boston, 1960

Marks, Robert W., *The Dymaxion World of Buckminster Fuller*, Reinhold, New York, 1960

McDougall, William, *An Introduction to Social Psychology*, L. Methuen, London, 1950

McLuhan, Marshall, *The Gutenberg Galaxy*, Signet Books, New York, 1969

Mead, Margaret, *Coming of Age in Samoa*, Modern Library, New York, 1953

Menninger, Karl, *Man Against Himself*, Harcourt, Brace & Co., New York, 1938

Meyerson, Martin, *Face of the Metropolis*, Random House, New York, 1963

Milner, Marion, *On Not Being Able To Paint*, International Universities Press, New York, 1957

Moholy Nagy, L. *Vision in Motion*, Paul Theobald, Chicago, 1947

Montague, Ashley, *The Biosocial Nature of Man*, The Grove Press, New York, 1956

Mumford, Lewis, *The City in History*, Harcourt, Brace & World, New York, 1961

Mumford, Lewis, *The Highway and the City*, Harcourt, Brace & World, New York, 1963

Munari, Bruno, *Discovery of the Square*, George Wittenborn, Inc., New York, 1965

Murphy, Gardner, *An Outline of Abnormal Psychology*, Modern Library, New York, 1954

Munari, Bruno, *Discovery of the Circle*, George Wittenborn, Inc., New York, 1965

Nehru, Jawaharlal, *The Discovery of India*, John Day Co., New York, 1946

Nordhoff, Charles, *The Communistic Societies of the United States*, Hillary House, New York, 1875

Panofsky, Erwin, *Meaning in the Visual Arts*, Doubleday, New York, 1955

Perry, John Weir, *The Self in Psychotic Process*, University of California Press, Berkeley, 1953

Petersen, William, *American Social Patterns*, Doubleday, New York, 1956

Pirenne, Henri, *Medieval Cities*, Princeton University Press, New York, 1956

Popper, Karl R., *Conjectures & Refutations*, Basic Books, New York, 1963

Power, Eileen, *Medieval People*, Barnes and Noble, New York, 1954

Rapoport, Amos, *House Form and Culture*, Prentice-Hall, New Jersey, 1969

Rasmussen, Steen Eiler, *Towns and Buildings*, Harvard University Press, Cambridge, Mass., 1951

Read, Herbert, *The Meaning of Art*, Pelican Book, London, 1951

Reik, Theodor, *Listening With the Third Ear*, Grove Press, New York, 1948

Report of the National Advisory Commission on Civil Disorders, Bantam Books, New York, 1968

Richman, Anthony H., *Science News*, Penguin Books, New York, 1953

Riesman, David, *Faces in the Crowd*, Yale University Press, New Haven, Conn., 1952

Rosenau, Helen, *The Ideal City*, Western Printing Services Ltd., Bristol, England, 1959

Rubin, Jerry, *Do It!*, Simon and Schuster, New York, 1970

Saarinen, Eliel, *The City*, Reinhold Publishing Co., New York, 1943

Schlote, W. & Becker, H.J., *Finlandia, Editzioni di "Communita-Milano,"* Milan, 1960

Scott, Geoffrey, *The Architecture of Humanism*, Scribner's, New York, 1969

Sert, Jose Luis, Rogers, E.N., *The Heart of the City*, Pellegrini & Cudahy, New York, 1952

Sharp, Thomas, Gibberd, Frederick, *Design in Town and Village*, Ministry of Housing and Local Government, M.S.O., London, 1953

Sherrington, Sir Charles, *Man On His Nature*, Cambridge University Press, New York, 1951

Sigmund, Paul E. Jr., *The Ideologies of Developing Nations*, Praeger, New York, 1963

Sirjamaki, John, *The American Family in the Twentieth Century*, Harvard University Press, Cambridge, Mass., 1953

Sitte, Camillo, *City Planning According to Artistic Principle*, Random House, New York, 1965

Sitte, Camillo, *The Art of Building Cities*, Rinehold, New York, 1945

Skinner, B.F., *Walden Two*, Macmillan Co., New York, 1962

Smailes, Adam, *The Geography of Towns*, Hutchinson, London, 1953

Smith, E. Baldwin, *Architectural Symbolism of Imperial Rome and the Middle Ages*, Princeton University Press, Princeton, New Jersey, 1956

Smithson, Alison and Peter, *Urban Structuring*, Studio Vista, London, 1967

Snyder, Gary, *Earth Household*, New Directions Pub. Corp., New York, 1969

Sorokin, Pitirim A., *The Reconstruction of Humanity*, Beacon Press, Boston, 1948

Sorokin, Pitirim A., *Social Philosophies of an Age of Crisis*, Beacon Press, Boston, 1951

Sprott, W.J.H., *Human Groups*, Penguin Books, New York, 1962

Sullivan, Louis H., *An Autobiography of an Idea*, Dover Publications, New York, 1956

Sullivan, Louis H., *Kindergarten Chats*, Wittenborn, Shultz, Inc., New York, 1947

Tse-Tung, Mao, *Quotations From Chairman Mao Tse-Tung*, Foreign Language Press, Peking, 1966

Tunnard, Christopher, *The City of Man*, Charles Scribner & Sons, New York, 1953

Tunnard, Christopher, *Gardens in the Modern Landscape*, The Architectural Press, London, 1938

Vernon, M.D., *A Further Study of Visual Perception*, Cambridge University Press, New York, 1952

Vitruvius, *The Ten Books of Architecture*, Dover Publications, New York, 1960

Wakefield, Dan, *Island in the City*, Citadel Press, New York, 1960

Watts, Alan W., *Psychotherapy East and West*, New American Library, New York, 1963

Whitehead, A.N., *Science in the Modern World*, New American Library, New York, 1963

Whitehead, A.N., *The Adventure of Ideas*, Macmillan Co., New York, 1933

Whyte, L., *The Next Development in Man*, New American Library, New York, 1950

Whyte, William H., Jr., *The Organization Man*, Simon and Schuster, New York, 1956

Wiener, Norbert, *The Human Use of Human Beings*, Doubleday, New York, 1954

Wilde, Oscar, *De Profundis*, Putnam, New York, 1905

Wingo, Lowdon, Jr., *Cities and Space: The Future Use of Urban Land*, Johns Hopkins Press, Baltimore, 1963

Wirth, Louis, *The Ghetto*, University of Chicago Press, Chicago, 1956

Wittkower, Rudolf, *Architectural Principles in the Age of Humanism*, Alec Tiranti, Ltd., London, 1952

Wood, Robert C., *Suburbia*, Houghton Mifflin Co., Boston, 1961

Wright, Frank Lloyd, *The Living City*, Horizon Press, New York, 1958

Yang, Martin C., *A Chinese Village*, Columbia University Press, New York, 1945

Young, J.Z., *Doubt and Certainty in Science*, Clarendon Press, Texas, 1951

Zimmer, Heinrich, *Myths and Symbols in Indian Art and Civilization*, Pantheon Books, New York, 1947

The *i press* Series on the Human Environment

The Ideal Communist City by Alexei Gutnov and other planner-architects from the University of Moscow.

World of Variation by Mary Otis Stevens and Thomas F. McNulty, Architects in Boston.

Toward a Non-oppressive Environment by Alexander Tzonis, Harvard University Graduate School of Design.

Systems and Models: The Completion of Urban Masses by Martin Kuenzlan, an architect from Berlin.

Forms of Communal Living by Gary H. Winkel and Renee Epstein.

Human Density: Studies of the Over-populated Society by Charles Correa, Architect and Planner from Bombay.

Socialist Solutions to Environmental Problems a collection of articles by architects and planners from Yugoslavia and other Eastern European countries edited by Vladimir Music, architect from Ljubljana, Yugoslavia.

Concepts for Continental Planning a collection of articles which will include studies by architects and planners in South America and Africa, and emphasizing the new settlements and decentralized planning concepts in mainland China.

Mary Otis Stevens.
the i press series.
Exhibition at NTU Centre for
Contemporary Art Singapore (2020)

Image Credits, pp. 177-184: *Mary Otis Stevens. the i press series*. (2020), curated by Karin G. Oen, NTU Centre for Contemporary Art Singapore. Courtesy NTU CCA Singapore.

Image reproductions from *World of Variation*, *The Ideal Communist City*, and the work of Mary Otis Stevens displayed in this exhibition appeared courtesy Mary Otis Stevens and MIT Museum Architecture and Design Collections.

some examples, such as the evolution of the Doric, Ionic, and Corinthian Orders in temple architecture, a refinement of proportion is achieved which endures as an aesthetic standard for succeeding centuries and civilizations.

The strength of the cultural forms seems to rely upon public attitudes and belief. Not surprisingly then, many lose their power to communicate. A good example is the "Tree of Liberty," an extremely provocative symbol during the American Revolutionary period but now

The Visualization of Cultural Forms

WORLD OF VARIATION

mary otis stevens – thomas mcnulty

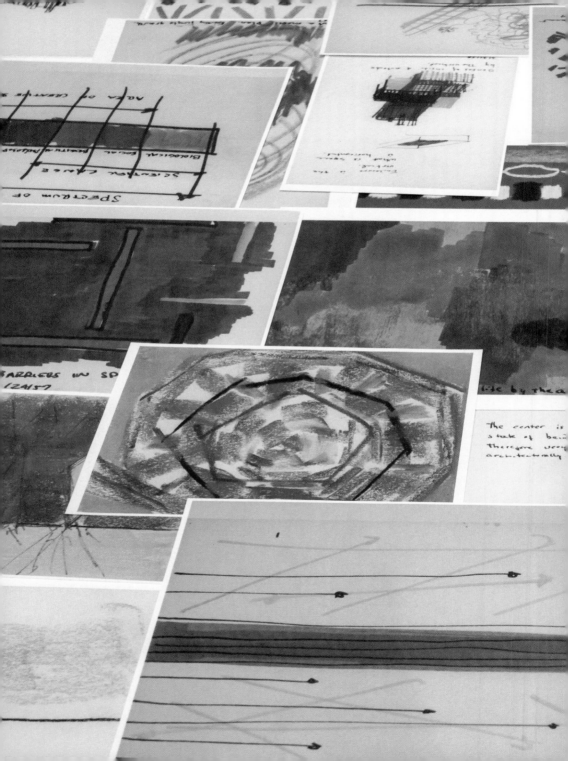

the i press series on the

THE IDEAL COMMUNIST

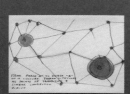

The materialisation
to thought and so c
of creation. Action
produce a thought.
another.

-Mary Otis Stevens

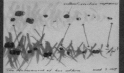

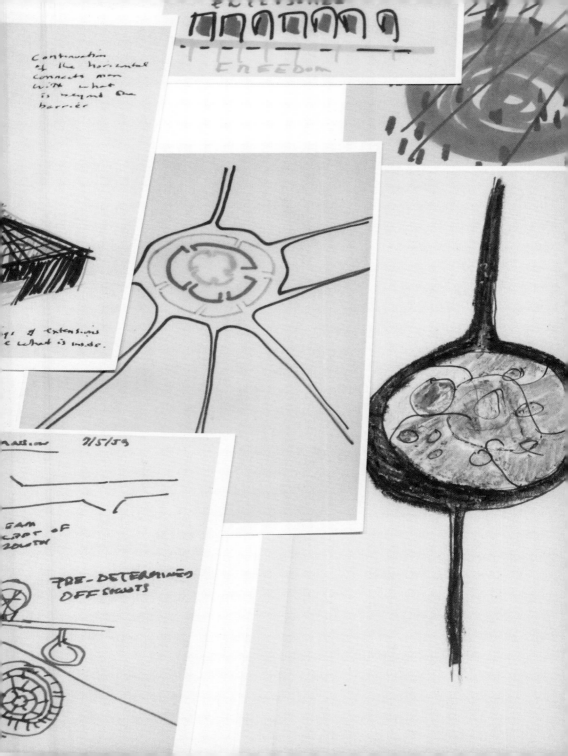

FREEDOM

Continuation of the horizontal connects man with what is beyond the barrier

g: of extensions e what is inside.

7/5/59

EAM ROT OF 20WTH

PRE-DETERMINED OFFSHOOTS

World of Variation
Facsimile 1

Mary Otis Stevens.
the i press series.
Exhibition at NTU Centre
for Contemporary Art
Singapore (2020) 176

Mary Otis Stevens.
the i press series.
by Karin G. Oen 186

Afterword
by Mary Otis Stevens 187

Editors' introduction
to the new edition 189

The Indeterminate Human
by Beatriz Colomina and
Mark Wigley 193

Conversations with
Mary Otis Stevens 195

Contributors' Biographies 203

Acknowledgments 206

Imprint 207

Karin G. Oen

Mary Otis Stevens.
the i press series.

NTU Centre for Contemporary Art Singapore's 2020 exhibition *Mary Otis Stevens. the i press series.* offered a deep dive into two of the i press titles: *World of Variation* and *The Ideal Communist City*. Thinking about how these books and their content could best be presented to new audiences, they were offered in multiple formats—original, enlarged and digital. *The Ideal Communist City* offers a way of thinking about mobility, access and equity, and social interaction in neighborhood planning, in direct response to suburban development and its focus on private spaces for family life. *World of Variation* explores the concept of variation as a fundamental component of life and design. In Stevens's words, "Only by variation can there be change. Only through contrast can one measure, appraise, and relate."[1]

This presentation showcased her sketches, drawings and designs that provide insight into concepts and visualizations around people, space, cities and society. In the context of the Cold War and American political activism of the 1960s, Stevens's work reflects her background in philosophy and her commitment to de-centralize hierarchies. The themes of active citizen participation in government, integrated planning and genuine risk-taking to make a substantial change in people's lives remain relevant and a crucial means of incorporating a social context into the practice of architecture and other activities affecting human wellbeing for each and for all.

Revisiting i press fifty years later in the form of an exhibition was not just a project to examine the rare out-of-print books, but a chance to reexamine the issues, architectural concepts and urban arguments presented by the authors and introduce them into the discussion and contemporary debates on planning sustainable architecture and urban development on local, national and global scales. As a preamble to the republication of these two books, the exhibition allowed for a special focus on the visual, spatial and social space that can be occupied by images and words in print media.

1   Mary Otis Stevens, "Notes on the Theme of Variation," (unpublished manuscript, November 24, 1969), typescript, MIT Museum Architecture and Design Collections.

Mary Otis Stevens
Afterword

"It is my opinion that the earth is very noble and admirable by reason of so many alterations and generations which are incessantly made therein."—Galileo Galilei

This opening paragraph from the original edition's preface seems as relevant today as at the time of its original publication in 1970.

> *Despite the tyranny and brutality of the present period, one cannot accept its forecast as the future of [humanity]. Or else [humankind] has no future. All who are involved with and love [our species] . . . will try to work for a last chance. The [architect/urbanist] can help to visualize the severe [societal] problems afflicting most societies today and the new potentialities and purposes that are emerging.*

Technological innovations continue to alter many basic living patterns; "*so that newer demands for urban facilities are not likely to be met by traditional procedures. Debate in older cities on issues such as centralized versus decentralized development and abandoning or resuscitating their cores illustrates some of the unresolved conflicts.*" In the twentieth century, cities became the geographical centers of global production, and this trend has intensified in the twenty-first.

Even if hypothetical proposals are seldom realized, they offer significant directives and options to individuals and communities of any size. As stated in the original edition: "*In a crowd the individual loses singularity—one becomes a unit, part of a mass . . . . Perhaps what really is at issue is the more complicated and sensitive matter of the scale of development and its influence on individual and group behavior. The precedent for defining a city in terms of numerical population has ancient roots. In a small group, a person has the potential of developing strong social relationships and playing responsible roles.*"

Discussing planning assumptions and attitudes is useful, especially for communities seeking appropriate forms for their new independence. Many societies were given cultural traditions by the powers that colonized them. *"These foreign frameworks will likely disappear and be replaced by ones more expressive of their inherent cultures."*

Part I articulates the philosophical approaches of the more detailed and specific design projects and ideas articulated in Part II and Part III. Design attitudes and purposes are examined for their relevance to both new and already developed world societies. A principal concern of Part I is investigating basic determinants of acculturation and speculating upon design frameworks for societies that can absorb growth rates without damaging sensitive environments.

Part II, the middle section of the book, is involved in present deficiencies in urban environments and how the architect/urbanist can help compensate for inevitable losses from cultural change. Proposals presented in Part II pertain particularly to urban areas in the United States, and formulate imagery of environmental change that is not manipulated but regenerative, inhering from events themselves.

Part III extends the scope of proposals and many of the ideas expressed in Part I and Part II. The concepts are highly experimental, envisioning the physical and social definition of whole societies, and therefore may be more applicable to communities in their formative stages than to those already well rooted.

The original text is followed by commentaries by internationally noted urbanists and design professionals in the environmental disciplines, including Pelin Tan, sociologist, art historian, professor at Fine Arts Academy, Batman University, and senior fellow at CAD+SR; Karin G. Oen, principal research fellow at the Centre for Asian Art and Design, School of Art, Design, and Media, Nanyang Technological University; Ute Meta Bauer, Founding Director, Centre for Contemporary Art, Singapore, and professor, School of Art, Design, and Media, Nanyang Technological University; Beatriz Colomina, professor of the history of architecture, Princeton University; and Mark Wigley, professor of architecture and Dean Emeritus, Columbia University.

There is more to be done in exploring the original text's directive: *"Consider the range of thought and experience available to the Athenian in the fifth century B.C., to the Roman in the third century A.D., to the Florentine and Venetian during the Renaissance, to the Parisian in the seventeenth century, the Londoner in the eighteenth, and the Viennese in the nineteenth."*

The need for empathy, observation and context allows one to understand and appreciate that every environment and each person differs in physical and social terms, but together they create a world of variation.

Ute Meta Bauer, Karin G. Oen, Pelin Tan

Editors' introduction to the new edition

The *i press series on the human environment* was originally published with New York-based publisher George Braziller fifty years ago, with Mary Otis Stevens and Thomas F. McNulty as co-founders and series editors. Over five years, i press offered five titles on architecture and urban planning that explored the social and cultural elements of the world we live in. The human environment has since experienced multiple revolutions and upheavals, as well as the acceleration and articulation of the climate crisis, technological capabilities that have contributed to the proclamation of the Information Age, and the sobering statistic that surfaced at the end of 2020 that the mass of human-made goods now exceeds living biomass on our planet.[1] Each i press book was modest in page count and price tag, intentionally designed to remain accessible to a wide public while simultaneously offering alternatives to the terrains of architectural theory and writing. Globalization, then an emergent discourse, has become a contested material reality. The i press imprint was highly creative and optimistic while also radical and critical in its politics, a characteristic clearly visible in the press's choice of subjects. As i press co-founder and pioneering American architect Mary Otis Stevens mentions in her statement written to accompany this reprint of *World of Variation*, there are certain elements of these texts that immediately date them and do not reflect current thinking and writing about culture and people. Phrases like "impassive peoples" and "once dormant cultures" that appear on page 3 of *World of Variation* sound archaic to our ears, but as Stevens herself noted, to attempt to retroactively edit or correct them is to introduce new inconsistencies and issues. Similarly, the treatment of the subject of prison redesign and re-configuration with "the absence of a punitive character" (p. 35) covered in "The Idea of Punishment" (pp. 33–40), might seem rear-garde given current urgent discussions of prison abolition and emancipatory justice. It should be noted that the text addresses the possibility of prison abolition while also acknowledging that "alternate types of protection and rehabilitation that might replace [prisons and mental institutions] are seldom explored," thus offering thoughts and suggestions for reform as a necessary consideration when abolition is not on the table. Other aspects of these books, including their very structure and design, speak to approaches and processes that are only now being embraced in the wider discussions of decolonization, organizational horizontality, diversity, equity and inclusion.

The republication of i press's first two titles, *The Ideal Communist City* (1971) and *World of Variation* (1970), is a project to introduce these books to new generations to reflect upon the continued urgency of the issues that they addressed. *The Ideal Communist City* offers a way of thinking about mobility, access and equity, and social interaction in neighborhood planning, in direct response to postwar suburban development and its focus on private spaces for family life. *World of Variation*, authored by i press co-founders Mary Otis Stevens and Thomas F. McNulty, explores the concept of variation as a fundamental component of life and design. In Stevens's words, "Only by variation can there be change. Only through contrast can one measure, appraise, and relate."[2]

The themes of active citizen participation in government, integrated planning and genuine risk-taking to make substantial change in people's lives remain relevant and crucial, insisting upon incorporating a social context into the practice of architecture and urban planning as they affect human wellbeing for each and for all. A conversation with Stevens included as new material to this edition of *World of Variation* fills in the context in which she and McNulty worked, translating postwar impulses toward collaboration, the rethinking of design processes and defining social responsibility into professional associations and projects, including the i press series. New contributions from leading scholars of architectural history and theory—Beatriz Colomina and Mark Wigley in the reprint of *World of Variation* and Ana Miljački in the simultaneously republished *The Ideal Communist City*—are instrumental in further situating the two reprinted i press editions, both as products of their times and archival resources for the present and future.

World of Variation presents design thinking that reveals the ongoing problematics of capitalist, consumerist urban spaces. Ideas and proposals of this book deal with human-centric spaces, arguing and bringing attention to the social interactions that form the basis of our collective daily life. It boldly addresses ideas on scale, the potentialities of spaces and a sophisticated understanding of the importance of nature for the vitality of built environments. Including humanist concepts of freedom that were largely constrained or minimized by design doctrines in the early twentieth century, *World of Variation* offers our twenty-first-century eyes surprising points of reference on the relationship of architecture to life.

Writing about i press in 1974 after the publication of the five editions, Mary Otis Stevens reflected that, "Although the authors and i press itself have tended toward a planning and architectural orientation, this background has not necessarily narrowed the contents or perspectives of either. It has, however, provided a point of departure for visualizing how urban and industrial processes affect and indeed radically shape and alter the lives of most people in most societies today."[3] The book starts with Galileo's phrase: "It is my opinion that the earth is very noble and admirable by reason of so many different alterations and generations which are incessantly made therein." Thus, the authors refer to this phrase that, from the beginning, signals to readers what *World of Variation* is all about: "the incessant variation." The sections of the book are: A Framework of Ideas, Architecture on a Social Scale, Architecture Beyond Cities. This structure details the desire to bring design into the adaptation of scales of human, communal life and nature of landscapes. The first chapter focuses on the variation of the effects of humans on the environment and provides a detailed analysis of the relationship between the variation of human nature and design. The second section investigates the social and communal scales within design, while the third section provokes visions of free action and mass movement in urban spaces and cities. Each chapter and sub-section bring forward the still-unsolved concerns in our current time of design thinking.

A fearless experiment and foray into new professional territory for two trained architects, i press remains an inspiration, encouraging us to remain curious and serving as a reminder that connectivity and collaboration are necessary for a collective future. As editors, we hope these books—republished in the context of the COVID-19 pandemic, when many aspects of our daily lives have been reconfigured—will spark new conversations and reveal the significance of constraints and limitations as necessary components of freedom and co-creation.

This project has been the work of many, beginning with the original i press editorial team of Mary Otis Stevens and Thomas F. McNulty in collaboration with the publisher George Braziller, and the authors of the five i press books. Mary Otis Stevens and Aliza Leventhal continue to represent i press, and it has been an honor to work with them to reintroduce these books to a new generation of thinkers and readers. Mary Otis Stevens has been generous with her time, and we are grateful for her willing participation in a series of interviews to generate the new material that accompanies *World of Variation*. Special thanks to Megan Chua for her assistance with transcribing these conversations for inclusion in this book and to NTU CCA Singapore's Sophie Goltz and Kong Yin Ying. This publication and the 2020 exhibition at NTU CCA Singapore were realized with the cooperation of the staff of the MIT Museum Architecture and Design Collections, including Gary Van Zante.

Jennifer Tran, and Jonathan Duval. James D. Graham provided valuable editorial insight in the publication's early stages. Beatriz Colomina and Mark Wigley's essay that accompanies *World of Variation* and Ana Miljački's essay to accompany *The Ideal Communist City* provide valuable context and commentary on the books and their place in architectural discourse, then and now. Kirsten Weiss and her team at Weiss Publications have played an integral role in sharing this work with a global audience. The editors additionally thank Maggie Yin, Ethel Baraona Pohl and Cesar Reyes Najera for their contributions to this republishing endeavor. Special appreciation and gratitude goes to Caroline A. Jones.

This publication is made possible with generous support from the Graham Foundation for Advanced Studies in the Fine Arts and additional support from NTU CCA Singapore, i press, the MIT School of Architecture and Planning Office of the Dean and the MIT Department of Architecture. But if not for the compassion, persistence, and resilience of Mary Otis Stevens, these two books would not have been in your hands.

1   Emily Elhacham, Liad Ben-Uri, Jonathan Grozovski, Yinon M Bar-On, and Ron Milo, "Global Human-Made Mass Exceeds All Living Biomass," *Nature* 588, no. 7838 (2020): 442–444, https://doi.org/10.1038/s41586-020-3010-5.

2   Mary Otis Stevens, "Notes on the Theme of Variation," (unpublished manuscript, November 24, 1969), typescript, MIT Museum Architecture and Design Collections.

3   Mary Otis Stevens, unpublished manuscript, September 12, 1974, typescript, MIT Museum Architecture and Design Collections.

Beatriz Colomina and Mark Wigley
The Indeterminate Human

A group of anti-war demonstrators in Boston determinedly march around the yellow cover of the 1970 book *World of Variation*. They are angry about violence and calling for change, yet peacefully stride towards the possibility of something better. Just a few trees and edges of buildings frame their continuous flow. We can sense that there is a kind of river of protestors stretching behind them and in front. The book itself is, as it were, suspended in this extended human flow. To open its soft cover is to enter a soft yet militant call for change. Mary Otis Stevens and Thomas McNulty ask for an architecture that lightly frames and fosters collaborative movement. Most of their one hundred or so images sketch some kind of motion that stretches beyond the limits of the frame. Architecture as such never appears, or appears only in being dissolved, depowering itself in order to empower those that pass through it. The real architecture of "the human environment" is the human itself and the most human thing about the human is variation. The book cannot be a manifesto, or at least not a typical manifesto, since the change it calls for is change itself. Its most insistent effect is to dissolve the restrictions imposed by conventional buildings and urban plans. Most of the work of the book is an undoing. Each drawing undoes a different constraint.

The need to be determinedly indeterminate shapes every detail of the book. There is a kind of egalitarian politics in the book. No drawing is allowed to be more important than another. No sentence rules over another. No drawing is ruled by a sentence or rules over it. This produces a kind of resolute flatness. The book can be read in any direction from any point. The sequence of images could be changed because it is not really a sequence. There is an ambiguity between descriptions of human activity and prescriptions for that activity. No single effect is imposed on the reader other than the insight that imposing anything singular on the human compromises the human. The very idea of the normal is challenged to treasure the "abnormal," "disturbed," "defective," "outsider," "rejects," "leftovers," and all those who "deviate." In the most literal sense, the book is counter-cultural. Then and now.

As hinted by the cover, the real frame of the argument is a horror of violence and a determination to resist it. The very first words of the book capture both revulsion and resistance: "Despite the tyranny and brutality of the present period, one cannot accept its forecast as the future of man." Likewise, the very last page refers to the "potentially self-destructive human world." The extended text in between these warnings explores ways for architects and planners to counter the inhumanity of humanity. Its optimism about the possibility of a less brutal future for the species embraces revolutionary destruction of restrictive spaces. The one time that words are superimposed as part of a drawing shows a sequence of quasi-architectural patterns from left to right with the one in the middle being a kind of explosion labeled "REVOLT" on the way toward a more hospitable because indeterminate pattern. The last drawing in the book shows the possibility to give "form and meaning" to an otherwise self-destructive humanity by offering a blurry "framework" of overlapping grids with some kind of explosion of human intensity erupting it. Architecture must undo itself in favor of an ever-changing diversity of human life, and life itself takes the form of undoing fixed architectures.

At the heart of this flat, non-hierarchical anti-argument that polemically refuses to linger on any one point, the book does slow down once to offer an extended account of a new kind of prison that no longer isolates one group of humans to protect society. On the contrary, a "thin membrane" offers protection from a hostile society and "transitional environments" foster reconnection. In fact, "the destructive tendencies in each prisoner" are treated as a form of "explosion" used "to build a new order." It is as if this possibility is meant to radiate out across the flat landscape of the book that effectively treats all conventional architectures and spaces as constraining prisons needing to be undone. The crime of architecture, of any fixed plan or object, is that it imprisons, constraining not just bodies but variations of behaviors and thoughts. The psychological spaces of "private sufferings," "fears," "anxieties," "nerve strain," "misery," "loneliness" and "breakdown" are architectural. Or, to say it the other way around, psychology must be the central focus of design.

This little book echoes the postwar philosophies of the so-called Team 10 group in so many ways, sharing their concern for less oppressive ways to host human communities, and likewise turning to Africa and Asia for vernacular and indigenous models for less restrictive patternings. The resonances with the thinking of Alison and Peter Smithson, Aldo van Eyck, and Giancarlo de Carlo are particularly deep. But postwar is not the same as anti-war. The final refusal to make a manifesto and the reluctance to privilege particular projects—or even draw particular projects, or draw them in a way they can be understood, or understood only one way—is unique. The commitment to the multiplicity and uncertainty of the human, and resulting transformation in the role of building, plan, architect and planner, is more in the spirit of the radical undoing of architectural constraint in Constant Nieuwenhuys's contemporary New Babylon project, which at a certain point challenged its own optimism for a new kind of unpredictable collectivity in the face of the relentless horror of the Vietnam War. As a parallel reflection on the indeterminate human, *World of Variation* is a radical work. After all, no human appears in this book all about the human in a series on the human environment. More precisely, no singular, static or recognizable human appears, only the shadowy flickering environments produced by ongoing human differences, interactions and interdependencies. A world of variation.

Conversations with Mary Otis Stevens

Conducted via video conferencing by the editorial team of this republication in June, July and August 2021, edited for brevity and clarity.

Karin Oen   Mary, please tell us about i press and the first two titles, *The Ideal Communist City* (1971) and *World of Variation* (1970), in the *i press series on the human environment*.

Mary Otis Stevens   There are striking similarities between the *World of Variation* and *The Ideal Communist City*. They both deal with the connection between concept and reality—the application of ideas in society. That is to me what all the i press books are about: it was an effort not to separate concepts from the world but to integrate concepts into the world as it is, and how it might be. Both *World of Variation* and *The Ideal Communist City* do this. *The Ideal Communist City* focuses mainly on the public realm, and *World of Variation* focuses on the mixture of individual and community and the balance between freedom and order. *The Ideal Communist City* is very different from the Soviet model or the Chinese model because it is not as autocratic or authoritarian. It also tries to involve individual freedom. The diagram on the cover shows how the authors connected the individual with the community.

KO   This project of reprinting these two i press books that have long been out of print is, in part, about returning to the archives and making these books available to a new generation. You've mentioned before that while you're interested in seeing these i press books back in circulation, you're not interested in a monograph on you and your work—can you tell us more about that?

MOS   I never have believed in "mono-" of anything. Everything has a context and there is no such thing as a single source of ideas or actions. In my opinion, that is a terrible notion that came with capitalism. I've never been a capitalist, I'm not a communist, I'm not an anything, but, basically, this idea of trying to take credit destroys the inherent multiplicity of contributors in human creation. "We're all in this life together," I keep saying over and over again in everything I do.

At the time of their original printing, the i press books didn't sell, and there was a good reason why they didn't sell—it was because the visual imagery was not what people expected. They expected realistic renderings and reproductions. But those images are loaded with cultural biases. How do you use or generate a visual language without that cultural baggage? That's what Gutnov and his group were trying to do! They were working as hard as we were on the same problem. They did use photographs but those were the most dated material in their book.

Developing an abstract visual language requires spontaneity, an openness to innovating ways of communicating ideas. Without its freshness, searches become sterile.

The i press books are not manifestos—it's very important to make this distinction. We were not making manifestos. We were expressing in contemporary verbal/visual language new approaches to conditions besetting the human environment.

Too much order is counterproductive to humankind and too little order results in anarchy. How to prevent these extremes and integrate opposing needs and aspirations into a greater context without destabilizing a community and causing chaos instead of equilibrium? That's really the theme that runs through most of the published i press books but there might be new themes coming up in the future.

Another theme in both these i press books is "freedom within a limited environment." Each book explores arenas where the public realm and private realm respectively dominates and the other is subordinate. How to integrate and rebalance them in a sustainable and human equilibrium? And also not to expect perfection. Humankind is imperfect, to begin with.

Everything is in flux, dynamic: life is movement. In *World of Variation*, that was Thomas McNulty's and my outlook: "architecture is the design of movement." Gutnov is saying the same thing, everything is moving. When it doesn't move, it's dead, it's stale. However, individuals and societies tend to cling to the past for security by building monuments. Nostalgia for a past moment in history is very different from memory and its functions to remember, record and interpret past events and the evolution of human knowledge.

Everything has its context and without the context, has limited applications. Einstein's e=mc2, just by itself doesn't mean anything more than its breakthrough in mathematical and physical relationships, but when the relativity of time and space is extended to the arts and society, then wow! There's a whole new view of existence, of the world. Connection is vital—whether it's an idea, action or object—for creative endeavors, in everything we do or think.

Ute Meta Bauer   Mary, you and Thomas McNulty worked with the publisher George Braziller, but he didn't invent i press. You and Tom, two architects, did. What motivated you to found i press, and what did you bring from architecture to publishing?

MOS Well, why not? For me, having a global outlook, one must question the use of borders. Why make borders if you don't need to? Obviously, societies, concerned about order and freedom, can't justify anarchy or oppressive regimes. That's what Galileo understood so well. Variation doesn't mean chaos. It means thinking and acting ecologically, following nature's sustainable systems. This perspective weaves through many of the i press books and drew me in 1968 to purchase the English language rights to *The Ideal Communist City* from Il Saggiatore in Milan. Written by Alexei Gutnov and colleagues at the University of Moscow, a Russian version was smuggled out of the Soviet Union in the same way as Leo Pasternak's *Dr. Zhivago*. That happened before the i press association with the New York publisher George Braziller.

Tom and I had no idea about the technical technicalities of publishing, but that was not a deterrence since George Braziller's firm produced the books and I benefited personally from his knowledge and wise advice over the five years of bringing out the five books in the *i press series on the human environment*. George was another free spirit and shared our goal to keep the dialogue open, invite notable authors in the design disciplines with all kinds of different opinions to author the verbal/visual essays.

UMB Architecture is traditionally so much about rules, and you're kind of unruly, you want to have things as you say, more open, more fluid, more borderless. I think it's very interesting that you worked within the constraints of architectural practice and architectural education, while also finding ways to bypass them.

MOS I don't think I'm very different from generations before the Industrial Revolution, with its societal as well as factory floor hierarchies, specializations and assembly lines. Nobody should be subjected to doing the same thing over and over again, day after day, year after year. Machines are programmed to do that. Humans are not. And I'm glad the COVID-19 pandemic has encouraged people around the world to rethink this issue. The upcoming generations, judging by comments of my grandchildren and their friends, are not going to put up with such treatment. They're saying, why should we, we're not born to be an X, Y or Z.

UMB Nevertheless, Mary, both the Constructivists and the Bauhaus attempted to make the transition from craft to machine fabrication, because they wanted to give everybody in a society access to products that otherwise would be too costly for the greater number if handcrafted. And that meant the mass production of goods and services. On one hand, this democratization of access has made daily existence more comfortable, but it has also led to today's consumer societies with their damaging impact on the planet's resources, climate and ecosystems.

The early designs by Tatlin and the whole Constructivist movement advocated machine fabrication that would provide material well-being where everyone is equal, but without a boss on top of the factory floor or ruler of the State. However, those goals proved unworkable and the same hierarchies took hold in the Soviet Union as elsewhere.

What I think is interesting about *World of Variation*: it is not a nostalgic book, it is not just looking backward in history for models, but in its text and imagery moves forward into the future. We need a holistic way to think people into a realistic future.

MOS   In any ecosystem, one is engaged in resolving opposites. In the societal context of these two i press books, mass production is viewed as being very helpful on some levels, and very oppressive on others. The approach is not only developing strategies for a long-term humane societal equilibrium but to work at other levels on specific issues and other timelines. When to address one? When do you focus on the other? And how do they integrate? And, and so instead of saying either, just say both—but in appropriate contexts.

UMB   Again, I think your point of view comes back to a "world of variation," one that cannot be ideological, has to be flexible, and it has to react to the specific situation and the particular condition.

Mary, we were also looking through your initial delineation of the *i press series on the human environment*, and you listed a number of projected titles, including topics like overpopulated societies and the postwar Japanese Metabolist movement that fused ideas about architectural megastructures with those of organic biological growth—it was an amazing list. You were thinking so globally on societal solutions to environmental problems—that could be a title right now!

Pelin Tan   Mary, I was curious about three topics regarding your practice. One is your activities with Architects for Social Responsibility. I am also curious about Design Guild, the multidisciplinary design firm that you founded in 1973 and engaged in socially oriented projects until 1992. The third topic I would like to focus on is your i press experience. How were the topics and the editorial decisions made? What was the process of deciding, for example, to publish *The Ideal Communist City*? How has the editorial process of i press evolved over the years since?

MOS   Well, let's begin with ASR, as we called Architects for Social Responsibility. It was patterned on Physicians for Social Responsibility, an international organization founded at the end of World War II by two prominent cardiologists, one in the US and the other in the Soviet Union, who responded to the threat of a nuclear war between the two adversaries by founding Physicians for Social Responsibility. And it was very successful.

In 1973, I joined the Boston Society of Architects and gravitated to ASR. Previously, Thomas McNulty and I, so involved with the Modern Movement, considered the AIA an outdated organization, so we never joined it. Like other professional societies, the AIA and its local chapters were—and still are—self-promotional and therefore avoid political and societal involvements. However, Sally Harkness, a far-sighted woman architect and a partner in TAC (The Architects Collaborative founded by Walter Gropius in 1945) and a longtime member of the Boston Society of Architects, was very much concerned about sustainability and energy conservation. Sally and I worked together in changing the mission of ASR from anti-war activities to promoting sustainable practice in the design disciplines. Our efforts not only succeeded locally, but nationally through the AIA's networks, which we used to distribute ASR publications and reach a wide audience for our reports on conferences and educational programs, including charrettes that we held at local venues. In this country, charrette means "a meeting in which all stakeholders in a project attempt to resolve conflicts and map solutions."

Our last and most successful charrette was on the future reuse of Fort Devens, a demobilized US Army base established during the First World War on land taken from four neighboring towns in Central Massachusetts: Harvard, Ayer, Lancaster and Shirley.

ASR formed an interdisciplinary consortium of design professionals and relevant consultants who volunteered for two years to meet regularly with representatives from the four towns' planning boards and governing agencies to develop a program for the three-day charrette. Over three hundred practicing design professionals, faculty members and students from the Boston area's architectural schools and educational schools attended. Supportive families in the four towns put them up in their houses. The charrette group divided into three teams. Each was challenged to come up with a five-year plan, a twenty-five-year plan and a one-hundred-year plan. And at each stage, the strategies had to build on what the preceding phase of the work had presumably accomplished.

Well, the charette and the proposals of the three teams were so popular and respected by all parties involved that in the actual legislative process of instituting Devens as an independent town, the charrette's sustainable guidelines were incorporated into the legal documents. I think it was the first town anywhere in the United States placing top priority on both environmental and societal sustainability. Perhaps the nineteenth-century utopian communities supplied a precedent, as they were cited in some of the manuals.

However, the history of Devens is a cautionary tale. For about ten, maybe fifteen years, it was a success story. Between 1991 when we held the charrette and the present day, people living in Devens and politicians in charge of its governance gradually abandoned its sustainable guidelines, incited by profit-making and our society's current trend to privatize the public realm.

The Devens case study demonstrates that ideal situations seldom last because local and outside factions opposing long-term goals for immediate benefits will form and subvert the public good. Nevertheless, it's very important to realize that the Devens guidelines are still there, embedded in its founding documents and history, and so, at any time, they could be reactivated.

Indeed, that is likely to happen in the near future because the site of this former army base sits on an aquifer. Ever since colonial times, the Nashua River watershed has brought water to as many as 800,000 households in surrounding communities. Accordingly, polluting the water would be devastating for all residents in the surrounding towns. And that has occurred in recent years. A private company was allowed to drain its used inks into the aquifer. Now the water is not potable to drink. Devens had to halt any more development. Even maintaining the existing status quo while cleaning up the mess is not succeeding.

PT   But does Devens exist anymore?

MOS   Well, the town does exist. That's the point, all the great infrastructure that the US Army had built and well maintained was very easily converted to peacetime development. Devens has an idyllic landscape setting, open fields and wooded groves, bird sanctuaries and conservation land. It is also directly connected to the major interstate highway network, providing rapid and reliable automobile and bus connections to Boston's international airport, its commercial, educational and cultural centers (without their high taxes and cost of living), as well as to a satellite airport and a nearby long-established regional city, Worcester, with Clark University, a highly ranked medical school, Amtrak railroad station, and commercial companies and industries. Devens, therefore, is within easy commuting distance to multiple job opportunities.

When the Army turned over most of its base to the newly formed town in 1992, the infrastructure had been well maintained and was easily converted to peacetime uses. There were churches of many religious affiliations and non-denominational chapels. The barracks housing troops easily transformed into offices for commercial and non-profit tenants. The base's school buildings and libraries were incorporated into the Massachusetts public school system; auditoriums and indoor recreational facilities were turned into community meeting centers; the variety of housing was retained and new units added as the need arose.

The problem was not implementing the renovation and reuse plans for the former army base or reconnecting Devens to the neighboring towns. The implementation of the charrette's architectural and planning concepts worked very well. The problem was how easily the sustainable guidelines were subverted because there were no enforceable rules to protect them. Devens was a micro version of what is happening everywhere on our planet. Without enforceable rules and regulations, it's not possible to prevent a majority or a minority in a community of any size from choosing and imposing a short-term gain at the cost of a long-term loss.

ASR experienced a similar fate. As the Cold War receded in American consciousness and the nation became preoccupied with other concerns, sustainability receded in favor of amenities of its "consumer society" and the privatization of its public domain.

PT   I guess the Cold War was a very effective period; it really influenced this process.

MOS   Yes, and its impact continues in new contexts. That's another reason why I think i press has continued to be relevant and its history compares in some respects with the ASR story. I think i press has continued to attract supporters because it was global from the very beginning. So, if conditions in one part of the world were hostile, another group in another part could take it on. That's the value of sustainable thinking and acting.

Design Guild, DG, as we called it, paralleled my involvement with ASR and with the Boston Architectural Center (BAC). Founded by local architecture firms at the end of the nineteenth century, it provided architectural training to their draftsmen, who were ambitious and aspired to become architects but couldn't qualify or afford the costs of attending traditional professional schools. The BAC was a night school. Anybody could walk in from the street and take its courses. The only payment its faculty received was a parking space and a $50 honorarium. To teach at the BAC, one had to be a qualified professional in the design disciplines, principally architecture, and submit an outline of a course they volunteered to teach. If enough students chose it, it would happen. If not, it wouldn't. So it was very Socratic. In other words, the BAC was like a street corner, the "stoa" where the likes of Socrates and other philosophically minded Athenians hung out.

At the same time, in the mid-1970s, I received two fellowships from the National Endowment for the Arts for my research on "vernacular traditions in American architecture." That undertaking resulted from the dramatic failure of the Modern Movement here in this country. Since our projects were so closely identified with it, Tom McNulty and I suddenly had no work, no clients. They all rushed to the postmodernists led by Robert Venturi, Denise Scott Brown, and other leading professionals in practice and teaching.

I responded by returning to my roots in a rural New York State community where people just followed building traditions that came with them when they emigrated to America. If they came from France, they built barns, houses, churches and town halls the way they did in their home countries—until after the War of Independence and the formation of the United States. Then all these building typologies began to merge, with intriguing results. As a child, I grew up near the original Shaker communities, whose way of life, products and means of their fabrication strongly influenced American culture into the twentieth century. In retrospect, historians have referred to the Shakers as the "American Bauhaus." It shaped my aesthetics at ten years old. Why did those buildings, those objects and tools look like that, and why didn't they conform to the prevailing lifestyles of the general culture?

These questions and the Shaker model of working also shaped Design Guild that some of my students, faculty colleagues and I formed in 1973. We would take on jobs and commissions that no traditional firms would or could, often because they were very difficult and complex, and usually not very profitable. The established Boston firms gobbled up all the good contracts, so we got very interesting jobs, many from grants and non-profits. The proposed reuse and renovation of Fort Andrews on Peddocks Island in the Boston harbor was very similar to ASR's Devens project. The sustainable guidelines for Peddocks Island were incorporated into the Boston Harbor State Park legislation. Unfortunately, Design Guild's endeavors, like ASR's, followed the same downward course.

Up to this point, in this country, long-term planning and goals are too easily subverted by subsequent administrations. That's an ongoing challenge also for i press. So, these three undertakings are all interrelated. I view this very positively because the strength of one, or the end experience of one, leads to the next, to a sort of interactive and creative recycling. And I think that's probably what we're experiencing with this project to republish, with new updates and commentary, *World of Variation* and *The Ideal Communist City*.

Contributors' Biographies

MARY OTIS STEVENS

Mary Otis Stevens, born in New York City in 1928, grew up in a rural upstate farming community where she experienced the sufferings and social injustices of the Depression years and formed her societal ideas. Influenced also by Buckminster Fuller, a family friend, Stevens early on began to think and act globally.

After graduating from Smith College with a BA degree in philosophy and art history, she gravitated to architecture, inspired by her visits to Europe's cultural centers, especially Paris. Entering MIT's architectural program in 1953, Stevens accelerated her course load to graduate in the class of 1956 with a BArch degree, allowing her to practice that profession. Always resisting straight lines as contradictory to life's flow, Stevens developed her curvilinear style in architectural projects.

While at MIT, Stevens met Thomas F. McNulty, who studied with Alvar Aalto and graduated with an MArch degree, class of 1949. He was immediately made a member of the faculty. Finding that they shared many views on both theory and practice, they teamed up in 1958 to form Thomas McNulty Architects, committed to new ways to practice and communicate their conceptual explorations.

That led them in 1965 to embody their view that architecture is "the design of human movement" on a pastoral site in Lincoln, Massachusetts, a Boston suburb. The Lincoln house was never a "house." The two undulating asymmetric poured concrete walls enclosed an open interior where only the bathrooms and kitchen were in fixed locations. Otherwise, it was a continuum allowing the inhabitants to identify living spaces and change them according to their particular requirements. This communal environment became increasingly resented by the townspeople, especially after all the worldwide attention and press coverage it received. After thirteen years, Stevens and McNulty sold the property to Sarah Caldwell, the noted founder and director of Boston Opera. She lived there for another thirteen years before selling it to a buyer who immediately blew it up and built a traditional New England residence on its ruins.

In 1968, Stevens and McNulty collaborated with György Kepes, founder and director of the MIT Center for Advanced Visual Studies, on *The City by Night* exhibit for that year's Triennale in Milan. During their site visits overseeing the installation, Stevens and McNulty took advantage of the opportunity to reconnect with their European colleagues, among them Giancarlo de Carlo, the Triennale's organizer. The outcome was the founding of i press, in association with the New York publisher George Braziller. In five years, they published five books. The first two, *World of Variation* by Mary Otis Stevens and Thomas McNulty, and *The Ideal Communist City* by Alexei Gutnov and colleagues at the University of Moscow, were intentionally paired.

Ending her partnership with Thomas McNulty in the early 1970s, Stevens returned to her quest for an American architecture that expresses its cultural roots. That led to her receiving two successive fellowships from the National Endowment for the Arts on "Vernacular Traditions in American Architecture." At the same time, Stevens began her involvement with the Boston Architectural Center (BAC), a non-profit night school providing a professional curriculum to students of any age, gender or background working by day in local architectural offices. Consequently, the BAC depended on a volunteer faculty. Many were also on the faculties of traditional architectural schools like Harvard and MIT.

UTE META BAUER

Ute Meta Bauer has since 2013 served as a professor, School of Art, Design and Media, Nanyang Technological University, Singapore, and as founding director of the NTU Centre for Contemporary Art Singapore (NTU CCA). From 2005 to 2013, she was an associate professor at the School of Architecture and Planning, Massachusetts Institute of Technology (MIT), where she was the founding director of the Program in Art, Culture and Technology (2009–12). For more than three decades, Bauer has been a curator/co-curator of exhibitions and presentations, connecting contemporary art, film, video and sound through transdisciplinary formats including documenta 11 (Kassel, 2001–02), the 3rd berlin biennale for contemporary art (2004) and the US Pavilion for the 56th Venice Biennale (2015), presenting artist Joan Jonas. She is a curator for the Singapore Pavilion, 59th Venice Biennale (2022), featuring artist Shubigi Rao, and a co-curator for the 17th Istanbul Biennale (2022) alongside David Teh and Amar Kanwar. She was an editor of *Afterall: A Journal of Art, Context and Enquiry* (2018–21). She recently edited *Climates.Habitats.Environments*. (2022), co-published by the MIT Press and NTU CCA Singapore.

BEATRIZ COLOMINA

Beatriz Colomina is the Howard Crosby Butler Professor of the History of Architecture at Princeton University and the founding director of the Media and Modernity Program at Princeton University. She writes and curates on questions of design, art, sexuality and media, and her writings have been translated into more than twenty-five languages. Her books include *Sexuality and Space* (Princeton Architectural Press, 1992); *Privacy and Publicity: Modern Architecture as Mass Media* (MIT Press, 1994); *Domesticity at War* (MIT Press and Actar, 2007); *Clip/Stamp/Fold: The Radical Architecture of Little Magazines 196X–197X* (Actar, 2010); *Manifesto Architecture: The Ghost of Mies* (Sternberg, 2014); *The Century of the Bed* (Verlag fur Moderne Kunst, 2015) and *Are We Human? Notes on an Archaeology of Design* (Lars Müller, 2016). Her latest books are *X-Ray Architecture* (Lars Müller, 2019) and *Radical Pedagogies* (MIT Press, 2022). She has curated a number of exhibitions, including *Clip/Stamp/Fold* (2006–13), *Playboy Architecture* (2012–16), *Radical Pedagogies* (2014–15), *Liquid La Habana* (2018), *The 24/7 Bed* (2018) and *Sick Architecture* (2022). In 2016, she was chief curator with Mark Wigley of the third Istanbul Design Biennial. In 2018, she was awarded an honorary doctorate by the KTH Royal Institute of Technology in Stockholm, and in 2020, she was awarded the Ada Louise Huxtable Prize for her contributions to the field of architecture.

KARIN G. OEN

Karin G. Oen is a principal research fellow at the Centre for Asian Art and Design, Nanyang Technological University School of Art, Design and Media (NTU ADM), and was recently deputy director, curatorial programmes for NTU Centre for Contemporary Art Singapore. Prior to that, she was associate curator of contemporary art at the Asian Art Museum in San Francisco. Oen holds a PhD in history, theory and criticism of art and architecture from the Massachusetts Institute of Technology, an MA in modern art history, connoisseurship and art-market history from Christie's Education and a BA with honors in urban studies from Stanford University. Engaged with the intersection of art, technology and culture, Oen is a global modernist whose curatorial practice spans the art and architecture from the nineteenth through twenty-first centuries.

PELIN TAN

Pelin Tan is a sociologist and art historian. She is the sixth recipient of the Keith Haring Art and Activism Award. Currently, she is a professor in the Film Department at Batman University Turkey, a senior research fellow at the Center for the Arts, Design and Social Research, Inc. in Boston and a research fellow at the Architecture Faculty of Thessaly University, Greece (2020–26). She is the lead author of the "Cities" report of the International Panel of Social Progress (Cambridge University Press, 2018). Tan participated in Chicago Architecture Biennial, 2019; Oslo Architecture Triennale, Oslo, 2016; Cyprus Pavilion, Venice Biennale of Architecture, Venice, 2016; Istanbul Biennial, Istanbul, 2015 and 2007; Biennale de Montréal, Montréal, 2014; and Lisbon Architecture Triennale, Lisbon, 2013. Tan is a guest curator of MAAT Lisbon in 2022 and co-curator of Urgent Pedagogies by IASPIS Stockholm. Tan collaborates with artist Anton Vidokle on essay films on the future society, and received the short film award by the Sharjah Art Foundation (AUB, 2020). She has written for publications including: *Designing Modernity Architecture in the Arab World 1945–1973* (Jovis, 2022); *Radical Pedagogies* (MIT Press, 2022); *Towards a Critical Architecture* (Spector Books, 2019); *Radical Geography Notebooks* (Athens, 2017); *Re-Production of Social Architecture* (Routledge, 2016); *The Tradition of Oskar Hansen* (Sternberg Press, 2014); *Urgent Architectural Theories* (GSAPP Books, Columbia University, NY, 2015); *Climates: Architecture and The Planetary Imaginary* (GSAPP Books & Lars Müller Publication, 2016) and *Swamps and the New Imagination* (MIT Press, 2023).

MARK WIGLEY

Mark Wigley is a professor of architecture and dean emeritus at Columbia University. He is a historian, theorist and critic who explores the intersection of architecture, art, philosophy, culture and technology. His books include *Konrad Wachsmann's Television: Post-Architectural Transmissions* (Sternberg Press, 2020); *Passing Through Architecture: The 10 Years of Gordon Matta-Clark* (Power Station of Art, 2019); *Cutting Matta-Clark: The Anarchitecture Investigation* (Lars Müller, 2018); *Are We Human? Notes on an Archaeology of Design* (written with Beatriz Colomina; Lars Müller, 2016); *Buckminster Fuller Inc.: Architecture in the Age of Radio* (Lars Müller, 2015); *Constant's New Babylon: The Hyper-Architecture of Desire* (010 Publishers, 1998); *White Walls, Designer Dresses: The Fashioning of Modern Architecture* (MIT Press, 1995) and *Derrida's Haunt: The Architecture of Deconstruction* (MIT Press, 1993). He has curated exhibitions at the Museum of Modern Art, the Drawing Center, Columbia University, Witte de With Center for Contemporary Art, Het Nieuwe Instituut and the Canadian Centre for Architecture. Most recently, he curated *Passing Through Architecture: The 10 Years of Gordon Matta-Clark* at the Power Station of Art, Shanghai (2019–20).

Acknowledgments

The editors wish to acknowledge the many individuals and institutions that have contributed to and supported this republication project over many years.

The original i press editors and publishers:
Thomas F. McNulty
Mary Otis Stevens
George Braziller

Current i press directors:
Mary Otis Stevens
Aliza Leventhal

The staff of the MIT Museum Architecture and Design Collections:
Gary Van Zante
Jennifer Tran
Jonathan Duval

Contributors:
Beatriz Colomina
Mark Wigley

Supporters and advisors:
Caroline A. Jones
James D. Graham
Ethel Baraona Pohl
Cesar Reyes Najera

NTU Centre for Contemporary Art Singapore staff:
Sophie Goltz
Maggie Yin
Kong Yin Ying
Megan Chua

This publication is made possible with the generous support of the Graham Foundation for Advanced Studies in the Fine Arts.

For additional support and donations, we thank:
NTU Centre for Contemporary Art Singapore
i press
MIT School of Architecture and Planning Office of the Dean
MIT Department of Architecture

Image Credits, pp. 177–184: *Mary Otis Stevens. the i press series* (2020), curated by Karin G. Oen, NTU Centre for Contemporary Art Singapore. Courtesy NTU CCA Singapore.

Image reproductions from *World of Variation*, *The Ideal Communist City*, and the work of Mary Otis Stevens displayed as part of the exhibition *Mary Otis Stevens. the i press series.* appeared courtesy Mary Otis Stevens and MIT Museum Architecture and Design Collections.

Color reproductions of the original materials reproduced in the World of Variation are available at http://www.worldofvariation.net.

Imprint

This publication has been made possible with the generous support of the Graham Foundation for Advanced Studies in the Fine Arts and additional support from NTU Centre for Contemporary Art Singapore, i press, the MIT School of Architecture and Planning Office of the Dean and the MIT Department of Architecture.

© 2022 the editors, Mary Otis Stevens, NTU Centre for Contemporary Art Singapore and Weiss Publications.

Editors: Ute Meta Bauer, Karin G. Oen, Pelin Tan
Managing Editors: Bianca Heuser and Maggie Yin
Copyediting (new text): Elise Ciez
Publisher: Kirsten Weiss
Design: Enver Hadzijaj
Printing: Kopa, Vilnius

All rights reserved. No part of this publication may be reproduced, stored in a retrieval system or transmitted in any form or by any means, electronic, mechanical, photocopying, recording or otherwise without the prior permission of the publisher. Every effort has been made to acknowledge the correct copyright of images where available. Any error or omission is unintentional and should be communicated to the publisher, who will arrange for corrections to appear in any reprint.

First Edition
Printed in Lithuania

NTU Centre for Contemporary Art Singapore
Block 6 Lock Road #01-09/10
Gillman Barracks
Singapore 108934
ntu.ccasingapore.org
ntuccacomms@ntu.edu.sg

Weiss Publications
Ohlauer Strasse 42
10999 Berlin (Germany)
www.weisspublications.com
info@weisspublications.com

Distribution
D.A.P. / Distributed Art Publishers
75 Broad Street, Suite 630
New York, NY 10004 (USA)
www.artbook.com
Tel.: +1-212-627-1999
orders@dapinc.com

ISBN: 9783948318178